M000310862

SAILING
THOROUGHBREDS

Happy Fathers Day
1999
Love
Jannett

ALSO BY
BEKEN OF COWES

One Hundred Years of Sail

The America's Cup

BEKEN OF COWES

SAILING
THOROUGHBREDS

Foreword by HRH The Princess Royal

Text by Tim Jeffery

THE HARVILL PRESS
LONDON

First published in 1998 by
The Harvill Press
84 Thornhill Road
London N1 1RD

www.harvill-press.com

First impression

Copyright © Beken of Cowes Ltd, 1998
Text copyright © Tim Jeffery, 1998

The authors have asserted their moral right

A CIP catalogue record for this title
is available from the British Library

ISBN 1 86046 345 2

Designed and typeset in Bembo
by Libanus Press, Marlborough, Wiltshire

Originated, printed and bound in Great Britain by
Butler & Tanner Ltd, Frome, Somerset

CONDITIONS OF SALE
All rights reserved. No part of this publication may be reproduced, stored in a retrieval system,
or transmitted in any form or by any means, electronic, mechanical, photocopying, recording
or otherwise, without the prior permission of the publisher

This book is sold subject to the condition that it shall not, by way of trade or otherwise, be lent,
re-sold, hired out or othewise circulated without the publisher's prior consent in any form
of binding or cover other than that in which it is published and without a similar condition
including this condition being imposed on the subsequent purchaser

Contents

Foreword
  by HRH The Princess Royal   7

Introduction   9

Part I: *Spirit of Tradition*   15

Part II: *Cruiser-Racers*   74

Part III: *Grand-Prix Elite*   110

Descriptions of the Yachts   177

Glossary of Terms, Races and Rules   205

BUCKINGHAM PALACE

The name Beken is synonymous with the sea. For as long as I can remember, Beken photographs have embodied the essence of sailing, encapsulating one of the great liberating, fulfilling and challenging activities that we can enjoy. No matter how often one goes to sea, there is always something more to learn.

Beken aficionados will revel in his new book. All sailors will delight in it. And for those who have yet to take to the water, what better stimulation could there be than the pleasure evident in these pages.

Anne

HRH The Princess Royal

President of the Royal Yachting Association

Introduction

I T CAME BY WAY of another great Cowes institution, the late Uffa Fox, and must owe something more than a nod of acknowledgement to John Masefield, but when Keith Beken wrote about his life in marine photography in the 1980s he wanted to title the book with one of Uffa's old sayings: *There's No Cure for Sea Fever*. In their wisdom, the publishers chose *The Beken File*, a bald title, devoid of any emotion. The French edition was little better: *Beken, ma vie*. Both missed an opportunity to bless Keith's book with words which encapsulate his work.

Beken photographs are portraits without equal and they owe much of that to the close relationship of a remarkable family dynasty to the sea and the vessels which used it as both highway and playground. Fashion photographers urge their models to see the camera as an extension of the photographer. They build up a relationship so that the model projects straight off the page, as if the camera wasn't there at all. The Bekens – for before Keith there was his father Frank, whilst for many years now Keith has run the business in tandem with his son Kenneth – have no means of cajoling, coaching and animating their subject. Their art comes from an innate knowledge of boats and the sea. They know the mood and movement of each and have the skill to combine them in a way which unfailingly pleases the eye.

The Bekens have been doing so for three generations. So much so that to connoisseurs a Beken image is unmistakable. Original prints of the early images are now highly prized by collectors. Even to those with but a passing interest in ships, yachting and the sea, a Beken photograph is the very epitome of what marine photography should be.

The Bekens are little short of being a national institution and deserve to be revered as such. By happy coincidence, their business was founded three generations ago in the reign of Queen Victoria when British yachting was in its infancy. It grew from the sport of kings and gentlemen to one that embraced Everyman and Everywoman. With it, British designers – the Fifes, G. L. Watson, Alfred Mylne and the Nicholsons – and British yachtbuilders became among the most eminent in the world.

Cowes, and especially its famous annual Regatta Week in August, became a magnet for all that was best in yachting. Through all the years, the Bekens have lovingly recorded it with thousands of images, still kept in their care. Performing a similar role in the USA, Morris and Stanley Rosenfeld built up an equally famous archive, their work overlapping principally when the Bekens began to travel to the America's Cup races, but whereas the Rosenfeld library has been renamed a Collection and installed with all attendant complexities of tight contracts, databases and administrators at the Mystic Seaport Museum, the Bekens maintain their archive in their shop.

Watching over this scene from the back will be Keith or Kenneth, for one or both are invariably in the shop, Keith perhaps tapping out a note on an old portable typewriter. This is not to say that there are no computers or word processors, but the pace of their arrival has been sedate rather than frantic.

Upstairs is a hodgepodge of large tables, a printing room, random shelving and box files, crammed with precious glass plates, negatives and transparencies. There are 100,000 black-and-white negatives, three-quarters of which are glass plate, ranging in size from 6 x 4 in to 15 x 12 in. Together they weigh seven tons. The colour images numbered 120,000 in 1997, but are increasing at the rate of 10,000 per annum. The bulk of business is with the older black-and-white stock, not simply because of the subject matter but because every print is a first-generation original. The large negative size ensures outstanding quality. Keith recalls seeing a print in Vancouver, hung in the yacht club in the full glare of the sun, which his father had printed fifty years previously. The picture looked as good as ever.

Alfred Edward Beken brought the family, including his eight-year-old son Frank, and the pharmacy business to Cowes from Kent in 1888. The pharmacy supplied the chemicals for the photography and Alfred Edward Beken dabbled in taking photographs ashore. But Frank's eyes were on the sea and by the time he was fourteen he was taking serious images afloat. As was often the case, a son followed the career chosen by his father and it was Frank who later decided that Keith would train as a pharmacist and take on the chemist's shop and photographic business. Keith's brothers were directed to banking and dentistry.

Come the more recent and liberated times, Kenneth chose photography of his own volition while his brother entered commercial diving and, latterly, computing. Today Kenneth's son, Jason, born in 1985, takes numerous photographs. As a schoolboy, he fancies flying. "At the very least, photography will be a hobby," says Kenneth of the prospect of a fourth generation Beken photographer.

Protecting all the negatives and film positives is a complex halon gas system. Water sprinklers would destroy the very thing they were trying to protect and the need for precautions does not need to be pressed home. There was a near miss in 1987 when an electrical fire created a lot of smoke but mercifully few flames. "It looked like a tandoori oven inside – a dark, evil glow," remembers Kenneth, who rushed to the shop when the burglar alarm went off and had finally melted after enduring six hours of smouldering heat. "Damage to the archive," says Kenneth, "would be a loss to maritime history."

The walls of the shop have the sepia tint of a classic Beken print, for shifting everything just to put on a lick of paint would be an operation of gargantuan proportions. Tucked away safely are the famous hand-built mahogany cameras which Frank and Keith designed to meet their singular need, brought across in 1970 from the other side of Birmingham Road when Keith decided that pharmacy was getting ever more complicated and that the maritime photography business could stand on its own feet at last. "For the first ninety years, the pharmacy supported the photography," Keith explains, "but we decided to split the two, sell off the chemist's shop and make a go of marine photography on its own."

The two businesses had earned an unusual distinction: Royal warrants from their majesties Queen Victoria and King George V for the chemist's business and one from HRH Prince Philip, Duke of Edinburgh, for the photographic work. The badges are displayed with manifest pride in the shop.

Frank's 1920s camera is a museum piece and like so much else of the Beken heritage and other elements of Cowes' historical past, it merits a permanent place on public display. The camera has been immortalized as the one with the mouth-operated shutter release. Frank would trigger the shutter with a rubber bulb, more commonly used for the remote operation of a tripod-mounted camera, held in his mouth, taking the practical view that not only would this leave his hands free to hold the fifteen-pound camera securely but that his body would naturally gimbal aboard the launch and provide a steady platform.

The camera superseded an earlier bellows affair which was not sufficiently watertight to take afloat and whose dim lens aperture of F8 and painfully slow shutter speed of 150th/sec meant that achieving pin-sharp images was exceptionally difficult. The wooden Mk1 camera had a 250th/sec shutter speed and a three-setting lens, which set aperture and focus to close-up, medium range and infinity. Operating it was as simple as using a box the size of a suitcase in a small boat can ever be. It took half a minute to change the glass plate and only twelve images at a time could be collected, so prepositioning of the launch, anticipation of events and the rare skill to compose and capture, with just one chance to get the shot right, were what set the Beken legend in motion. At first, not even a powered launch was used, rather a rowing dinghy which was kept at the bottom of the garden of the family house beside the Medina. Far from being a hindrance, the weight of the camera was a virtue, for its mass, unlike the lighter bellows camera, served to steady it. The boat was made by a cabinet-maker from the J. Samuel White shipyard.

In the 1960s, Keith designed his Mk2 version of the camera, essentially building a box around an adapted Zeiss camera, especially to cope with the demands of colour film, which in its early days was very slow, requiring a larger aperture lens. Colour film then was rated at 8ASA: how different from the 200ASA or 400ASA film we take for granted today. In British conditions, there was just enough reliable bright light to use the original Mk1 camera. The discipline of right-first-time photography remains today. While all around them you will see fast inflatable boats, bearing photographers with long lenses and motor-driven cameras, seeking more action-orientated images, you can often detect the Bekens holding back, waiting for the clutter to clear, before taking their images. Keith and Kenneth probably spend more time on the water and take fewer exposures than any other marine photographers.

"We are very much of the style where you choose your subject carefully, move around it until it looks perfect and then, and only then fire the shutter," Kenneth explains. "This has much to do with our past when we could make a maximum of forty exposures in a day using glass plates," adds Keith. "That's because we did not have time to change the slide for another shot if the subject was moving at fifteen knots, as it took us thirty seconds to change the plate. So it trained us to take the best picture. Each one had to be right first time." Even today, while other photographers afloat rattle off film after film in their motor-driven 35mm format bodies, Keith and Kenneth shoot selectively with their Hasselblad and large-format cameras. As a consequence, 99 per cent of what is shot produces a usable original image.

Over the years, yachting photography has changed, both stylistically, becoming more graphic- or action-orientated, and technically with the opportunities afforded by faster film, longer, faster lenses and routine use of helicopters. Throughout, the Bekens have remained steadfastly faithful to their own style. Their calendars have retained the same character for twenty-seven years and remain huge sellers. "Other photographers have come onto the sailing scene and added their own interpretation," concedes Kenneth, "but there is no doubt that if a person is asked who will take the finest picture of their yacht, then the Beken name will be to the fore."

There is a right place to shoot from, asserts Keith. "I've always maintained that there is one angle from which it is best to take any boat, be it a liner or a yacht. There is one perfect angle, and I think Kenneth and I know how to find it. We seem to correlate." Sensing exactly where an individual vessel's sweet spot is, is second nature to the Bekens. The style and indeed the relationship between father and son appears to be so symbiotic that the only way to differentiate between Keith's work and that of Kenneth is to look for the tiny telltale film marks which show whether a photograph was shot on the former's Rolleiflex or the latter's Hasselblad.

The Beken look is created using a standard 80mm lens, a modest focal length compared with the 400mm, 600mm and ever longer lenses used by others. Used in a studio ashore, it would be referred to as a portrait lens as it offers the most faithful representation of the subject without any optical tricks of distortion. "We use a standard lens on our cameras," explains Kenneth, "and the boats to zoom in or take wide angles."

Whilst Frank started with a rowing dinghy before progressing, in 1928, to a Meadows-powered launch with particularly sweet lines, built by Ned Williams just up the Medina from the Beken home, in the 1960s Keith used a Campbell Christina as his photo boat. This was replaced by his own Windy 28-footer and the second of two Boston Whalers, which Kenneth uses today. Happily for a family business which thrives on tradition, the original launch has came back. It was sold to make way for the Campbell Christina in the 1960s and the last that had been heard was of its sorry demise, burnt by the Sea Scouts on the beach. Not so: it was found submerged on a mudbank in Yarmouth in west Wight. An enthusiast had begun restoration, but found the operation too daunting and so rang the Beken shop. Keith and Kenneth paid the costs of the work done to date and then set about finishing the project off. Her launch party in 1998 is also a birthday party: the vessel's seventieth.

The family name is thought to have Flemish origins. A gravestone dating from William of Orange's time, with Beken on one side and Beacon on the other, has been traced by a family member. Van der Beken may have been the original name but it is a pleasant irony that a family which later became inexorably linked with the sea could have had Beacon as its Anglicized name. At least similar pronunciation keeps that link alive.

Selecting from the Beken collection demands an appreciative eye and a steely nerve so that hundreds of thousands of images can be whittled down to the 124 plates in this, the latest compilation. It features yachts photographed by Keith and Kenneth over the past decade, their hunting ground being the Solent, Caribbean and Mediterranean. The images are arranged in three categories: *Spirit of Tradition*, *Cruiser-Racers* and *Grand-Prix Elite*.

The *Spirit of Tradition* yachts may be as old as the last century and restored to their original glory or among the most recent launchings, but all are unique, individually designed and built yachts. They may race, but they are not designed to any contemporary rating rules, though many were built to such rules in the past.

Amongst the *Cruiser-Racers* are the dual-purpose yachts, built for both speed and comfort, many series-produced yachts from some of the world's top builders, as well as some former elite Grand-Prix boats whose days as greyhounds are over.

Finally, the *Grand-Prix Elite* are precisely that: contemporary, custom-designed racing boats built with the latest technology, created to suit various rules and formulae whose express purpose is speed and success on the race course, with all other considerations secondary.

I

II

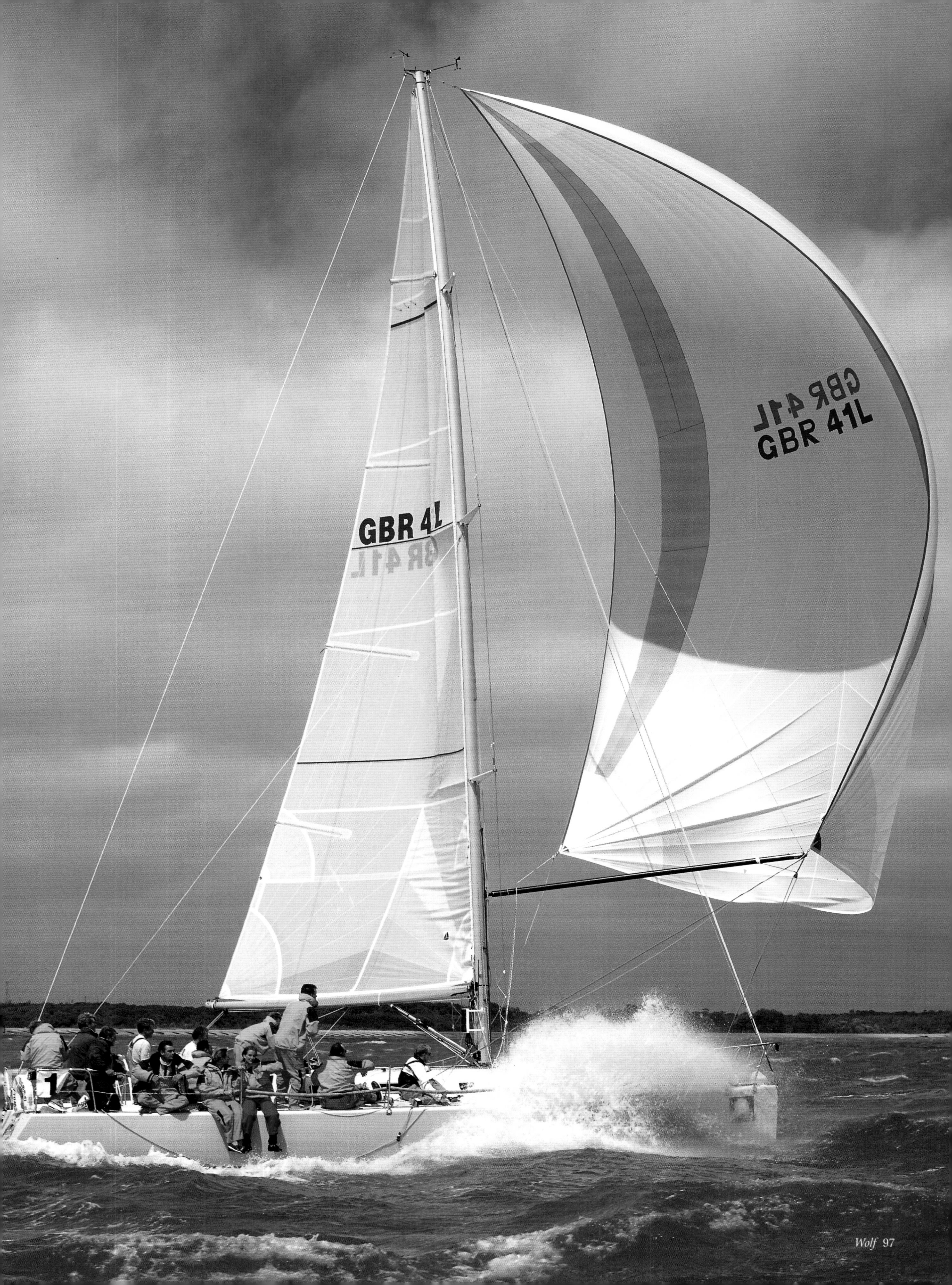

III

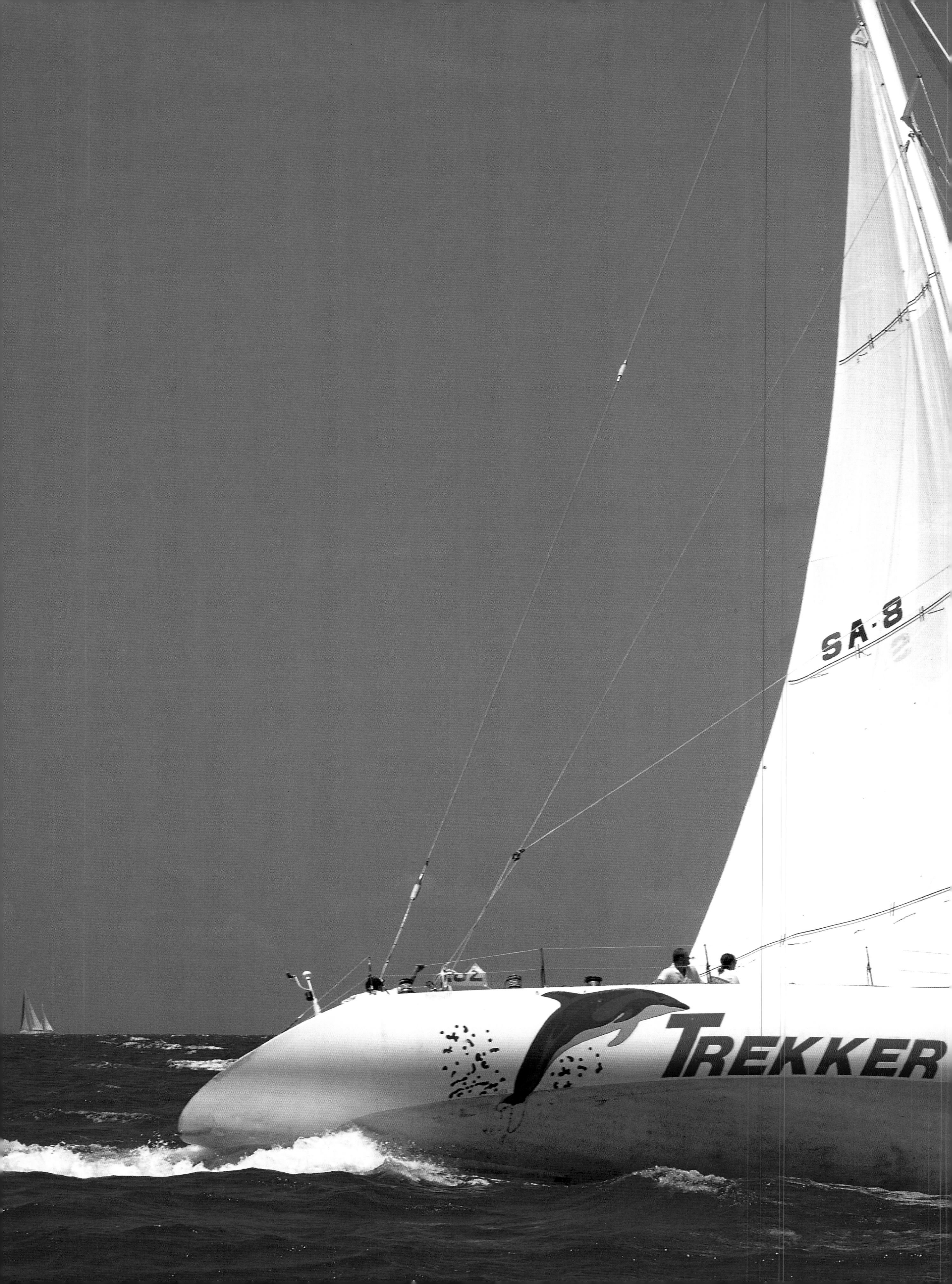
SA-8
TREKKER

Equation 149

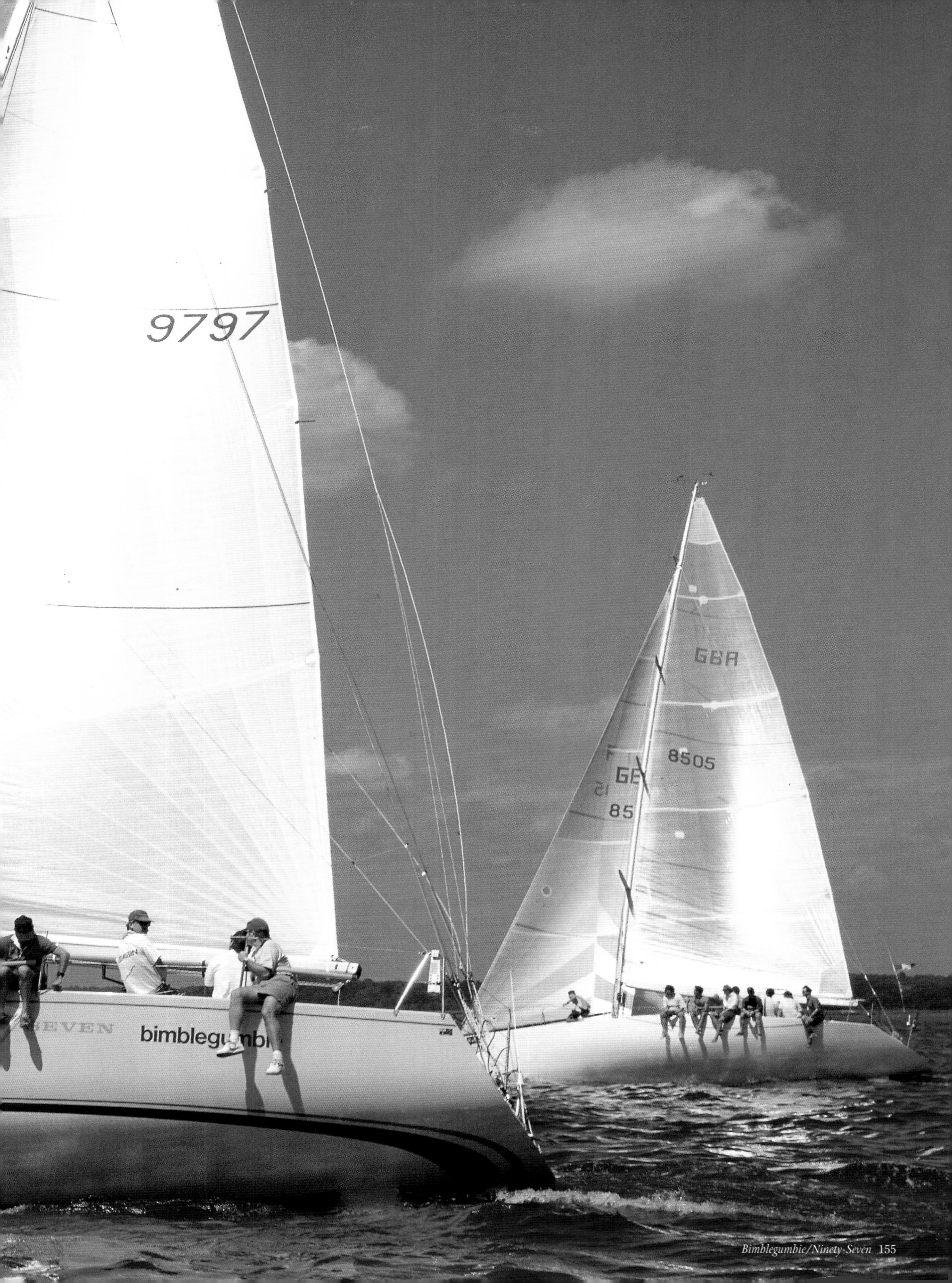
9797
GBR
8505
GB
85
SEVEN
bimblegumbi

Pen Duick page 17

A little deception helped save *Pen Duick* from falling into the wrong hands. During World War II when the Tabarly family had lain the boat up in a mud berth near Benodet, the Germans were told her keel was iron and not lead. And when in postwar France Guy Tabarly decided he could no longer keep the Fife 50-footer he'd bought in 1939, the 15-year-old Eric Tabarly wilfully made the yacht seem unattractive to would-be purchasers.

His father relented but the family finances were no better off, so *Pen Duick* languished in another mud berth near La Trinité. In 1952, the boat's condition was so bad that Guy Tabarly considered selling her just for the value of the lead, but Eric prevailed upon his father. About to enter the Navy, he would save enough to repair the yacht. Recognizing his son's love for the yacht, Guy Tabarly gave her to Eric. He became her 14th owner. In 1956, Eric returned from Saigon, where he'd been a Navy pilot, with money in the bank, only to be devastated when told that *Pen Duick* now needed a total rebuild.

That was beyond the young flier's means, so, with the aid of six women from the local oyster beds, Tabarly used the old hull and a fortnight's good weather to laminate seven layers of glassfibre. Lovely though the pitch pine planking might have been, the hull needed internal bracing to pull it back into shape. Back in 1959, glassfibre was a new fangled material, and *Pen Duick* was the world's longest grp hull. The maiden sail, her first since 1947, was traumatic; *Pen Duick* being comprehensively dismasted. Tabarly found an old fishing boat mast and planed it down to size and for three seasons, 1960–63, raced her hard in Royal Ocean Racing Club events. This was her second stint of racing. Built near Crosshaven for Adolphus Fowler of the Royal Cork YC in 1898 the yacht raced until the late 1920s under a succession of owners.

Winning the 1964 Singlehanded Transatlantic propelled Tabarly into the limelight as France's most famous sportsman and for 21 years his beloved *Pen Duick* (Breton for Coal Tit) was laid up once more. This time the plywood deck and superstructure had rotted through so Raymond Labbé of St Malo carried out a complete rebuild and by 1989 *Pen Duick* was sailing again, at her best for more than 50 years.

LOA	49ft 6in	15.10m
LWL	32ft 10in	10.00m
Beam	9ft 7in	2.90m
Draught	7ft 3in	2.20m
Displacement	22,400lb	10,100kg
Sail area	1,750sqft	160m²
Designer	William Fife III	
Builder	Gridiron Works, Carrigaloe, Ireland	
Launched	1898	

Vagrant pages 18–19

Graduation presents do not come much finer than this. Harold Vanderbilt was given this 106-foot gaff schooner by his family in 1910. *Vagrant* was created by Nathaniel Greene Herreshoff, a prince among designers, and built at the famous Herreshoff yard in Bristol, Rhode Island, with whom the Vanderbilts had strong business links.

There is not a line which does not please, due in part to Herreshoff's practice of designing by eye from models. You can almost picture the "Wizard of Bristol" holding the model and rotating it slowly to check and check again every line for its form, function and beauty. The proof is *Vagrant*'s progress through the water. The wake is clean and she creates a very flat wave-form.

Vanderbilt raced her straightaway, winning the Bermuda Race.

She remained on the Eastern Seaboard under new ownership and a new name, *Queen Mab*, and after World War II headed for the West Coast and raced in nine consecutive Transpacs, 12th being her poorest result. She nearly came to an inglorious end in the Caribbean. Unloved, she was dismasted and almost sank until found in Antigua in 1985 by British businessman Peter de Savary. A £1.5 million extensive restoration was carried out by Antigua Slipway, with a new rig from Harry Spencer of Cowes and an interior from Terence Disdale. Remarkably Spencer's Ben Bradley visited the yacht only once to measure up before the new rig was made. She is now in Japanese hands.

LOA	106ft 5in	32.50m
LWL	59ft 0in	18.00m
Beam	18ft 0in	5.60m
Draught	11ft 5in	3.50m
Displacement	157,451lb	71,420kg
Sail area	4,305sqft	400m²
Designer	Nathaniel Greene Herreshoff	
Builder	Herreshoff Shipyard, Bristol, Rhode Island	
Launched	1910	

Imagine page 20

Imagine is one in a string of large sailing vessels stemming from the collaboration between Lymington-based British designer Ed Dubois and the Auckland yard, Alloy Yachts International. The first was the 122-footer *Aquel*, which was Dubois' first superyacht, designed in 1986, the same year that his *Full Pelt* One Tonner was top yacht in the Sardinia Cup.

Imagine was launched by her enthusiastic Swiss owner in 1993 and since then she has been around the world twice. Twelve months after she hit the water, *Imagine* took part in La Nioulargue in St Tropez, having won the Big Boat Series which immediately preceded it. Two years later she was in San Diego for the America's Cup and was second overall in the Demi Tasse series of races staged especially for the large performance yachts which had migrated to California for the Auld Mug.

Such mega-yacht races have become a speciality for *Imagine*. She returned from San Diego to Auckland's Waitemata harbour for a race against the 121-foot *Atlanta*, another Dubois/Alloy creation owned by Georgia attorney Billy Payne, organizer of the 1996 Atlanta Olympic Games. The yachts raced for a US$10,000 wager, paid to a children's charity. Of all the large performance

cruisers Ed Dubois has designed, *Imagine* is among his favourites. While his office created the interior space planning, the styling was done by Agnès Comar of Paris, her first yacht commission.

LOA	110ft 3in	33.60m
LWL	89ft 3in	27.20m
Beam	25ft 6in	7.80m
Draught	10ft 8in	3.30m
Displacement	262,080lb	119,000kg
Sail area	4,811sqft	477m²
Designer	Ed Dubois	
Builder	Alloy Yachts International, Auckland	
Launched	1993	

Stormy Weather page 21

When famous Boston designer John G. Alden saw *Stormy Weather* out of the water for the first time, he said: "There is not one line I would change on that boat." Compliments do not come greater than this. Launched in 1934 by the Nevins yard on City Island, New York, for Philip LeBoutillier, president of the Best department stores business, *Stormy Weather* cemented the growing reputations of Olin & Rod Stephens. Their firm, Sparkman & Stephens, went on to become the most famous yacht designers of the century. The young men had made an impact when in 1931 *Dorade*, Olin's first design, won the first Transatlantic Race and then the Fastnet.

Several other designs followed, but *Stormy Weather* was the next hugely successful ocean racer, repeating in 1935 *Dorade*'s Transatlantic and Fastnet victories, once again with Rod Stephens as skipper. The impact of the Stephens' yawls was such that they soon eclipsed the Alden schooners as the definitive passage-makers. *Stormy Weather* appears a progression from *Dorade* but the differences were profound: she was two feet longer and broader, carried 200 square feet more sail area and softer sections forward. Her string of successes saw her win the 1936 Transpac race and every Miami-Nassau race between 1937 and 1941, her dominance of the East Coast mirroring *Dorade*'s on the West.

Stormy Weather's return to Cowes in 1995 under her new owner Paul Adamthwaite was only the latest stage in a full life.

LOA	53ft 11in	16.43m
LWL	39ft 9in	12.11m
Beam	12ft 6in	3.81m
Draught	7ft 11in	2.40m
Displacement	44,800lb	20,321kg
Sail area	1,332sqft	123.70m²
Designer	Sparkman & Stephens	
Builder	Henry B. Nevins, New York	
Launched	1934	

Altair page 22

"My dear Fife, on the day of my 44th birthday I am giving myself the treat of sending you the definite order for the yacht. I am sure she will be a lovely ship and will do you great credit all over the world." So wrote Captain Guy MacCaw in 1930 to the then 73-year-old William Fife III, commissioning the design for the 129-foot gaff schooner *Altair*, one of the famous designer's last and greatest creations.

She was to have been a world cruiser, but in the event, *Altair* never ventured further than France's Biscay coast, yet through a string of caring owners and a magnificent restoration by Southampton Yacht Services in 1986, she remains as one of the finest, most original and universally revered 1930s yachts.

Altair was bought by Viscount Runciman from MacCaw for Solent racing in 1933, then passed to Sir William Verdon-Roe in 1938 before undertaking mine clearance service during World War II, after which she was decommissioned and bought by a Portuguese. Her next owner, the Spaniard Miguel Sans Mora, cherished *Altair* so deeply that she has retained her remarkable condition. Built to Lloyd's 100 A1, she remains in class to this day.

Her current owner, a Swiss gentleman, is an avowed Fife aficionado. He saw *Altair* in Barcelona and persuaded Miguel Sans Mora to part with her. Then came her two-year SYS restoration, so thorough that *Altair*'s decks and internals were removed and numbered before re-assembly. The teak- and oak-framed hull was found to be remarkably sound, though the iron floors inside were badly corroded. A new deck was built, but the mahogany panelling of the accommodation has remained in excellent shape and much of the original equipment, from electrical switches, lights and taps, to the Oregon pine and spruce spars, Thomas Reid windlasses and original anchors, and even the Chernikeef instruments in the deck house, could be used after refurbishment.

LOA	129ft 7in	39.52m
LWL	77ft 9in	23.71m
Beam	20ft 4in	6.20m
Draught	13ft 2in	4.00m
Displacement	360,640lb	163,000kg
Sail area	6,000sqft	558m²
Designer	William Fife III	
Builder	William Fife & Son, Fairlie, Scotland	
Launched	1931	

Shamrock V   page 23

Only ten J-Class yachts were built between 1929 and 1937. Neither before nor since has there been another class to touch the heart so deeply. Few yachts combine size and power – they ranged between 129 and 135 feet in length and displacement spanned a staggering 128 to 166 tons – with such feline poise. Their lines were lithe and their graceful bow and stern overhangs, sweeping sheerlines and towering rigs, the very epitome of elegance.

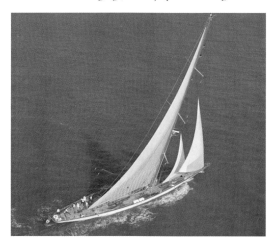

It's easy to think of the America's Cup as a vehicle for promoting the rich and famous, the Peter de Savarys, Alan Bonds and Bill Kochs of the world, yet competing for the Cup has always served someone's purpose beyond winning a race. When *America*'s owners brought her over to race against the British in 1851 it was to make money by betting on the outcome of her races, and Sir Thomas Lipton used the Cup to popularize his tea in the USA.

No other man has challenged for the Cup five times and come away empty handed but that was the sad fate of Sir Thomas Lipton.

Shamrock V was both the first J-Class yacht built and Lipton's last challenger. She is also the only wooden J-Class yacht still sailing, thanks to a string of owners who have always cared for her. After Lipton came the British aviation pioneers Sir Thomas Sopwith and Sir Richard Fairey. Mario Crespi installed the bird's-eye maple interior after World War II before she passed on to an Italian, Piero Scanu, who returned her to her original builders, Camper & Nicholson, for a complete rebuild. Then in 1986, the Lipton Tea Company bought the yacht and donated her to the Museum of Yachting in Newport, Rhode Island, where she came under the care of Elizabeth Meyer, owner of *Endeavour*.

LOA	120ft 0in	36.60m
LWL	87ft 0in	26.50m
Beam	19ft 9in	6.06m
Draught	15ft 6in	4.75m
Displacement	327,040lb	148,000kg
Sail area	9,200sqft	854m²
Designer	Charles E. Nicholson	
Builder	Camper & Nicholson	
Launched	1930	
Rebuild	J-Class Management 1988–90, Newport, Rhode Island	

Eugenia V   pages 24–5

Rejoice in *Eugenia V*, for her Italian builder, Sangermani, is one of the few true artisan yards remaining in the world which is still run as a family business. Three generations of the Sangermanis have built boats at Lavagna on Italy's Levante coast between La Spezia and Genoa, each yacht more a piece of furniture than a machine for sailing. "Our boats need very special owners," says Cesare Sangermani, grandson of the yard's founder. "The labour

is very expensive and it is very difficult to find the quality of wood we need, so we have to charge a lot of money to build a boat. There are a lot of rich people today," but he adds wistfully, "there are not a lot of gentlemen."

In *Eugenia V*'s case, her owner is a lady, Mrs Romilda Bollati de St Pierre, a well-known Turin society figure, and the Starnina Shipping Company, who have kept the yacht in immaculate order since her launch in 1968. Sangermani's time-served craftsmen planked her hull from mahogany over oak frames, with an iroko interior, teak decks and sitka spruce spars. There was a time when this was the common currency for a top-drawer yacht, but today, such vessels are rare. Sadness has visited the yacht, for the owner's husband, the prominent Italian government minister Signor Bisagalia, died aboard *Eugenia V*.

The yard was started almost as a hobby when Dorin Sangermani built a boat for each of his sons, Cesare and Pietro, who turned yachting into a business. Cesare Jr joined the yard full-time in 1966 and despite no formal education as a naval architect has designed many of the more famous Sangermani yachts. He is a reluctant designer, enjoying the creation of a yacht but not the detailed draughtsmanship, preferring the yard's clients to employ an outside naval architect to draw up the construction details. "I think that a boat must have a father who is the shipyard and a mother who is the architect," he says. Sparkman & Stephens and Laurent Giles are among those designing yachts for Sangermani with Baron Edmund de Rothschild's *Gitana IV* the yard's most famous vessel. *Eugenia V* is a Phil Rhodes design and in her early years raced in events such as the Giralgia. In more recent years, she has attended classic yacht events in Italy (Imperia and Porto Cervo) and France (La Nioulargue). *Eugenia V* was Philip Rhodes' design No. 82 and built as double-ended steel centreboarder for Mr J. E. Ottaviano.

LOA	71ft 8in	21.91m
LWL	50ft 0in	15.25m
Beam	18ft 0in	5.49m
Draught	9ft 7in	2.95m
Displacement	168,000lb	76,200kg
Sail area	3,257sqft	302.20m²
Designer	Philip L. Rhodes	
Builder	Sangermani, Lavagna, Italy	
Launched	1968	

Alzavola   page 26

Elegant she probably was not. Effective, she most certainly was. *Tern IV* was Claud Worth's seminal yacht, which really established the role of the Corinthian amateur making open sea passages for pleasure. True, others had cruised before Worth, but often they were gentlemen travelling aboard their yachts which were run by paid hands and their professional skipper and mate.

Momentum picked up at the end of the 19th century. In 1880 Arthur Underhill founded the Cruising Club (later Royal Cruising Club) in Britain. In 1895–8 American Joshua Slocum sailed alone around the world, while fellow American Thomas Fleming Day popularized and promoted amateur cruising and racing through his magazine *The Rudder*. Worth mirrored his efforts in Britain. An RCC member, he was a driving force in establishing the less exclusive Cruising Association but perhaps his most profound and influential impact was through his two books *Yacht Cruising* (1910) and *Yacht Navigation & Voyaging* (1927). Without the forcing ground of racing, cruising boat design was an undernourished branch of the sport.

Worth designed *Tern IV* himself because "Mrs Worth desired more accommodation". Every facet of the yacht is described in the minutest detail in *Yacht Navigation & Voyaging*. "Besides the lines of the vessel and general construction drawings, I prepared a very full specification and made detail drawings to scale of all the ironwork and every detail of construction and equipment," he wrote. "The work took nearly a year and was done mostly between five and eight in the morning."

Of *Tern IV*'s cruises, Worth wrote with the same exacting thoroughness of every facet of cruising under sail. Even today his books remain standard works, for though technology and techniques have moved on, values have not. *Tern IV* became Mrs Noel McGrigor Phillips' *Sea Swallow* in the 1930s and nowadays sails under Italian ownership as *Alzavola*. Enrico Zaccagni's yacht has chartered in the Caribbean as well as participating in such events as the classic yacht regattas in Imperia and Porto Cervo.

LOA	62ft 0in	18.89m
LWL	49ft 5in	15.08m
Beam	13ft 6in	4.14m
Draught	8ft 0in	2.44m
Displacement	85,120lb	38,600kg
Sail area	2,000sqft	185.80m²
Designer	Claud Worth	
Builder	Philip & Son, Dartmouth, England	
Launched	1924	

Sensation   page 27

The qualities of a Ferrari car were what *Sensation*'s owner was after when the 110-foot sloop was commissioned from Ron Holland in the late 1980s. She had to look fast, even at rest, have excellent sailing performance, be no slouch under power and echo the aesthetics of contemporary powerboat design in her superstructure. As with other large Holland yachts, *Sensation* helped pioneer ideas that are now the norm for such vessels. Her deck layout was remarkably unencumbered by sail-handling gear upon her launch, thanks to collaboration with Peter Powell of Seaway Winches who created reel winches which were concealed in and under her superstructure.

To avoid the performance compromises of a furling mainsail, *Sensation* carried a conventional, fully-battened sail which was not only more efficient but allowed a significantly lighter mast as well. She was also Ron Holland's first large yacht to carry over the knowledge gained in New Zealand's America's Cup challenge in 1987 in Fremantle when he was part of a design team including Bruce Farr and Laurie Davidson. Part of their research was into low-resistance, low-draught, low-centre of gravity keels, all highly desirable factors in big boat design.

Sensation was built by Sensation Yachts in Auckland, the old Thackery Yachts which had been restructured under new ownership in 1987, with this as the first of many projects. She was also one of the earliest projects for London stylist Andrew Winch, who had set out on his own after many years in Jon Bannenberg's hugely influential Chelsea studio.

Since launching, *Sensation* has sailed extensively in the US, Caribbean and Mediterranean and, in 1996, her white topsides were repainted dark blue.

LOA	110ft 7in	33.75m
LWL	85ft 5in	25.35m
Beam	24ft 27in	7.40m
Draught	11ft 1in	3.44m
Displacement	257,600lb	117,000kg
Sail area	5,274sqft	490m²
Designer	Ron Holland Yacht Design	
Builder	Sensation Yachts, Auckland	
Launched	1991	

Zaca a te Moana   pages 28–9

Erroll Flynn bought *Zaca* from the US Navy in 1945, removed the two 20mm cannon, put a rig back and changed her battleship grey topsides to a white suitable for a yacht. *Zaca* was now ready for her film debut, which she made in 1947 with Rita Hayworth and Orson Welles in *The Lady from Shanghai*.

Zaca reflected her owner's glory days and decline; from entertaining the likes of Prince Ali Khan and Prince Rainier when *Zaca* came to the Mediterranean in 1950, to Flynn's death amid drink and debt after which the yacht belonged to the Villefranche shipyard. *Zaca* (Samoan for peace) was Flynn's last yacht, his life and reputation ruined by scandal, not all justly laid at his door. "I had lost the will to live," he said at the time of buying *Zaca* after rape charges against him (brought by two girls who

had been aboard his previous yacht *Sirocco*) had collapsed. "I knew I had lost. I already bore a label which society would never let me lose." Subsequent owners came and went until beyond hope and beyond restoration, she was sunk in 1991.

Like a phoenix from the ashes an entirely new yacht with a 124-foot deck was created in the image of the original *Zaca*, a fitting reward for a yacht originally designed by Garland Roach and built by the San Francisco Bay yard of Nunes Brothers of Sausalito in 1930. Before her war service, owner Templeton Croker made two circumnavigations. The new *Zaca* was built in the Netherlands by Amstel BV in 1992 to designs of Olivier van Meer. She has all the latest systems and equipment with a particularly light and airy maple and bird's-eye maple interior.

LOA	143ft 7in	43.80m
LWL	124ft 7in	38.00m
Beam	23ft 6in	7.20m
Draught	14ft 0in	4.28m
Displacement	392,000lb	177,800kg
Sail area	8,772sqft	815m²
Designer	Olivier F. van Meer	
Builder	Amstel BV, Netherlands	
Launched	1992	

Stealth   pages 30–31

Superlative yachts would never exist without imaginative owners and for *Stealth* we have to thank Italy's most famous industrialist, Gianni Agnelli, for this extraordinary yacht. Her name might be *Stealth* and she might be black as pitch, but this German Frers-designed 93-footer is probably the most eye-catching sailing yacht afloat in the world today.

The name and colour for the hull, mast, deck house and most unusual of all, the sails, came from Snr Agnelli himself and she follows in the footsteps of his 120-foot *Extra Beat*, another Frers design, but built from aluminium by Abeking & Rasmussen. Like her, *Stealth* aims to be nothing more than an exceptionally fast day boat. Green Marine of Lymington built her in record time, using a full carbon-fibre prepreg system engineered by SP Systems & Technologies. The result is a boat which is light, stiff and taut as a drum. With her colossal rig, *Stealth* is all about reducing sailing to its fundamental pleasure: she is fast, swift to accelerate and has great sensitivity. Providing the power to carry the huge sail plan is a deep, slender strut keel, specially fabricated from steel in Italy, which carries an 18-ton lead bulb at its tip.

There is little to slow the boat down in the way of unnecessary accommodation. The fit-out is very spartan, though beautifully executed, amounting to no more than a small owner's cabin, a large galley, chart table and centreline seating. A 50-foot grand-prix race boat probably has as much, except a decent galley.

In styling, *Stealth* echoes the International America's Cup Class, though it is longer and very narrow forward, with dart-like hollow waterlines. Her home port is Port Vauban in Antibes, close to Snr Agnelli's base in Turin. In light to medium winds, she canters around the Riviera faster than the wind speed, sailing upwind at 11 knots in a 9–10 knot wind and at very close angles.

LOA	93ft 1in	28.45m
LWL	80ft 2in	24.44m
Beam	19ft 8in	6.05m
Draught	16ft 0in	4.90m
Displacement	62,720lb	28,400kg
Sail area	3,799sqft	353m²
Designer	German Frers	
Builder	Green Marine, Lymington, England	
Launched	1996	

Velsheda   page 32

The numbers of the J-Class tell the story. Only ten were built, six in the USA, four in the UK, and they raced for a mere eight seasons bracketed by the Great Depression and World War II. Only three survive and *Velsheda* is the last to undergo restoration. The America's Cup was their playground, though of the four British Js, *Velsheda* was the only one not to race for the famous trophy.

Velsheda was designed and built by Camper & Nicholson in 1933 for the Woolworth's magnate W. L. Stephenson for racing in the Solent and on England's east and south-west coasts and he named her in honour of his three daughters: Velma, Sheila and Daphne. It was an idea which clearly appealed for when Bill Stephenson had Campers build him a 456-ton motor yacht in 1937, he used the last letters of their names to construct *Malahne*.

Successful in home waters, *Velsheda* was never held in the same reverence as *Endeavour I* and *II*, failing to match their aesthetics because of overlapping steel plate topsides. Her 90-ton lead keel was hacked off during World War II and she has had a chequered history since. She spent 31 years laying in a mud berth on the River Hamble near Southampton, until she was refloated in the mid 1970s and passed through several hands. A partial rebuild saw her bird's-eye maple joinery destroyed. In 1978–9 south-coast businessman, Terry Brabant, bought *Velsheda* and for much of the 1980s she sailed with concrete ballast, a reduced sail plan, plywood interior and leaky decks. No matter, Brabant had breathed life into her until someone else came along with the means to do the job properly.

A new owner made a deal with Camper & Nicholson at Gosport, Portsmouth Harbour, to restore her but that fell through. After two and half years of litigation and another change of ownership, *Velsheda* was hauled out in early 1996 at Northam, the former C&N site in Southampton. A huge task lay ahead to update her, make her suitable for sailing to venues all around the world and to comply with tough Lloyd's Register and Marine Safety Agency rules. Some 80 per cent of the hull metal was replaced. Watertight bulkheads were installed as was 60 tons of new lead ballast and her first engine. John Munford designed deckhouses and accommodation to suit her age but in one giant forward-looking stride, a new carbon fibre mast was ordered from Carbospars. The day when *Velsheda* meets *Endeavour* and *Shamrock V* is one to be savoured.

LOA	127ft 0in	38.83m
LWL	83ft 0in	25.30m
Beam	21ft 2in	6.40m
Draught	14ft 11in	4.57m
Displacement	320,326lb	145,290kg
Sail area	7,541sqft	700.65m²
Designer	Charles E. Nicholson	
Builder	Camper & Nicholson, Gosport, Southampton	
Launched	1933	

Sintra   page 33

Depending on whether Myrna Snider's daughter and mother are with her there might be as many as three remarkable ladies aboard *Sintra*, but usually there is just Myrna Snider herself, living on the yacht since 1979. "This is my sole home," she says. "When the youngest of my four children left home for college, I decided to runaway to sea. I thought: what a shame to own a yacht like this and not use her. I am not the type of person to sit at the dock drinking cocktails."

For nearly 20 years, *Sintra* and Myrna Snider, have been on the move. The Atlantic has been crossed twice and visits made all around the Mediterranean and the Baltic. The Panama Canal has also been transitted twice, with one cruise going right through Polynesia and as far as Si-pan, *Sintra* only turning around when advised that pirates had made the Malucca Strait unsafe. And she has been up and down the North American east coast from Florida to Nova Scotia. "It's been an incredible experience because we have been exposed to so many different cultures," Myrna Snider says, who must have spent more Christmases at sea than ashore. Even in port and during refits, whether in Trinidad, Toulon, Gosport, Savannah or Antibes, *Sintra*'s owner lives aboard.

Heavily built in steel by Abeking & Rasmussen, *Sintra* has an unmistakable rig: wishbone ketch. The only change over the years has been replacing the original sitka spruce spars with aluminium ones, while skipper Martin Thomas, who bought the vessel on behalf of the previous owner to Myrna Snider, added a bowsprit. This not only looks right on *Sintra*'s bow but she had ample stability to carry the extra power and the addition has greatly enhanced the yacht's sailing ability. "She's a wonderfully strong boat and performs so well," says Myrna Snider standing watches whilst passage-making and rolling her sleeves up to keep *Sintra*'s extensive brightwork varnished. Passers-by on the dockside often mistake her for one of five crew. "If they ask who the owner is, I reply: 'I'm not at liberty to say but I do know she's a fantastic woman!'"

LOA	107ft 0in	32.60m
LWL	68ft 0in	20.70m
Beam	21ft 0in	6.40m
Draught	11ft 6in	3.53m
Displacement	320,400lb	137,000kg
Sail area	6,000sqft	557.40m²
Designer	Loudendorf	
Builder	Abeking & Rasmussen, Germany	
Launched	1959	

Ticonderoga pages 34–5

Big *Ti*'s place in history is due to her epic battle with Kees Bruynzeel's van der Stadt-designed *Stormvogel* in the 1965 Transpac race from San Francisco to Honolulu: *Ticonderoga* won the duel for line honours by 1,000 yards after 2,225 miles – the stuff of legend. Though a 1936 ketch with a long shallow keel, *Ticonderoga* enjoyed a racing life as long as it was successful. Few yachts have been as widely campaigned, mostly under Robert Johnson's ownership from 1963 onwards. Following her Transpac success, she took line honours in the 1965 Sydney-Hobart and China Sea Races and 1966 Transatlantic and Skaw

Races – 50,000 miles of racing in 12 months. Her Miami–Nassau record set earlier in 1940 stood in the books for 26 years and even then only three minutes was shaved off it. In all, *Ti* is said to have held some 30 records.

Keen students of yacht design will recognize something of *America* and 19th-century US packet schooners in *Ticonderoga* and quite deliberately so. L. Francis Herreshoff gives five reasons why this should be: cheap building costs because of the straight keel; shallow draught without a penalty in leeway; good interior volume thanks to the long floor line; dry ride thanks to flared bows; excellent seaworthiness with slow motion.

Perhaps *Ticonderoga* was a lucky yacht from the start, for she virtually launched herself from the Quincy Adams yard in Quincy, Massachusetts in August 1936 when her cradle disintegrated and ejected the skipper into the water. Designed as *Tioga II* by Herreshoff for Harry E. Noyes of Marblehead, she seemed an unlikely greyhound. Refrigeration, central heating, bath tub and two radio telephones were uncommon in the 1930s and none of them light weight fixtures. Her first race record was set in 1938 over the modest 171-mile New London–Marblehead course. Noyes was killed in a 1941 air crash and his yacht did her war service for the US Coastguard. It was her second owner, Alan Carlisle, who changed her name to *Ticonderoga* as the Noyes' family wanted to retain *Tioga*. Another three owners intervened before Robert Johnson embarked on her second racing career, among them John Hertz of the car rental family.

By the end of the 1960s her racing days were largely over and she cruised and chartered extensively, having been replanked below the waterline and her frames and backbone repaired. Latterly, Californian Robert Voit has owned her. In 1990 he brought her to Southampton Yacht Services where a new deck and extensive repairs to her framing and topsides were made, ensuring the legend lives on.

LOA	72ft 0in	21.90m
LWL	68ft 0in	20.70m
Beam	16ft 0in	4.90m
Draught	7ft 9in	2.40m
Sail area	2,897sqft	269m²
Displacement	107,290lb	48,768kg
Designer	L. Francis Herreshoff	
Builder	Quincy Adams, Massachusetts	
Launched	1936	

Endeavour page 36

One of the world's most achingly beautiful yachts, *Endeavour* has been restored to all of her 1930s glory, and beyond it, by American Elizabeth Meyer. But in between her custodianship and *Endeavour*'s launch in 1933 for British aeroplane pioneer Sir Thomas Sopwith, Charles Nicholson's greatest creation suffered all manner of indignities. Sopwith applied aviation technology to his America's Cup challenger. Among *Endeavour*'s innovations were electronic wind instruments, efficient two-speed winches and a clever welded steel mast. No other challenger came as close to winning the America's Cup during the New York Yacht Club's 132-year defence as *Endeavour* in 1934. She was faster than *Rainbow* but ultimately, Harold Vanderbilt and his tactician Sherman Hoyt outfoxed Sopwith who shortly before had sacked his professional crew over a pay dispute. "The America's Cup was on its way back to England," wrote Vanderbilt of the event.

Laid up for the war, *Endeavour* endured a sorry decline. Sopwith sold her to banker Herman Andreae. A scrap merchant called Kerridge bought her in 1947, having already bought *Endeavour II*, but she was saved by Richard Lucas, owner of the Crableck Yard, on the brink of her destruction and was laid up on the Hamble alongside *Velsheda* and *Lulworth*. Lucas' widow sold

Endeavour for a token sum to the American Museum of Yachting, but a plan to return her to the USA fell through and she passed to the Maritime Trust. Taken to Cowes, she sank in the River Medina above Cowes in the 1970s. Patched up, she remained unloved. John Amos bought her for £10, towed her to Southampton and Calshot, but the enormity of the undertaking defeated him. He spent seven months chipping out the concrete ballast which had been poured into her. Salvation came in the form of Elizabeth Meyer, who bought *Endeavour* in 1984 and moved her to the famous Royal Huisman Shipyard in Vollenhove, Netherlands, for complete restoration and modernization. The cost of the fabulous result, when *Endeavour* was relaunched five years later, stood at £10 million – not such a staggering sum, for the yacht must have cost Sopwith around £1 million.

She sailed for the first time in 50 years on 22 June 1989. Though a show stopper, *Endeavour* is always on the move, racing in regattas such as La Nioulargue and taking charter guests in the Caribbean, Mediterranean and North America. Miss Meyer, niece of the *Washington Post*'s owner Katherine Graham, has invested huge emotional commitment not just to *Endeavour* but *Shamrock V* too, saving two of the famous J-class yachts for posterity. It is fitting, therefore, that the transom of *Ranger*, the last and greatest J of all, adorns *Endeavour*'s saloon.

LOA	129ft 8in	39.58m
LWL	88ft 2in	26.88m
Beam	22ft 3in	6.78m
Draught	15ft 7in	4.78m
Displacement	365,120lb	362,880kg
Sail area	13,802sqft	1,282m²
Designer	Charles E. Nicholson	
Builder	Camper & Nicholson	
Redesign	Gerry Dijkstra	
Rebuild	Royal Huisman Shipyard, Vollenhove, Netherlands	
Launched	1933 and 1989	

La Desirade page 37

La Desirade now resides in Thailand, taken there by her fourth owner, Frenchman Daniel Gudeman, who bought the yacht from François Spoerry, the architect famous for creating the Port Grimaud marina village in the Gulf of St Tropez.

It was François Spoerry who gave the yacht the name of his previous yachts, *La Desirade*. Before that she had been known as *Galaxis Beta* and before that *Galaxis Alpha*. She was originally a German-owned yacht, sixth in a series of nine 72-foot aluminium alloy ketches designed by Dominique Presles and built by Chantier Navale de Biot near Nice. The Presles 70 series were pitched at the charter market but one, *Fernande*, turned out to be a remarkably successful racing boat. Her second place in the 1979 Bermuda-Lorient two-handed race, behind the big trimaran *VSD*, made a name for her in France, reinforced when she won the monohull division in the La Baule-Dakar and Quebec-St Malo races in subsequent years. *Fernande* is now sailing in Antarctica from her base in Ushuaia, the main differences between her and *La Desirade* being interior and deck layout.

LOA	70ft 4in	21.45m
LWL	55ft 8in	17.00m
Beam	16ft 10in	5.15m
Draught	10ft 0in	3.05m
Displacement	60,480lb	27,400kg
Sail area	2,906sqft	270m²
Designer	Dominique Presles	
Builder	Chantier Navale de Biot, France	
Launched	1981	

Jolie Brise pages 38–9

Here is a yacht which underscores Britain's entire ocean racing history. There had been the great Atlantic races in 1870, 1887 and 1905, plus five races to Bermuda from Brooklyn between 1905 and 1910, but nothing so organized on the European side of the Atlantic. Until 1925. Englishman Weston Martyr was living in New York when he took part in the 1923 and 1924 Bermuda Races and came back to Britain to promote the idea of offshore racing. "I was shocked to discover that our yachtsmen had practically never heard of an ocean race and were apparently content to do their racing around short courses in sheltered water," he wrote.

With Evelyn George Martin, Martyr proposed a race from Cowes around the Fastnet Rock, off Ireland's Cape Clear, and back. News of it was carried in the *Morning Post* and *Sunday Express*, the latter expecting "important entries from America".

They never materialized, but a fleet of seven did, among them Martyr's own *Jolie Brise*. She was a Le Havre pilot boat but that was not exceptional. Only two entries had been built as yachts, the others were Colin Archer types or Bristol Channel pilot cutters. Some six days 14 hours later *Jolie Brise* won both line honours and handicap victory and Martyr and Co. kept up their momentum by founding the Ocean Racing Club, which by 1930 had gained its Royal prefix. British offshore racing was born.

Martyr found *Jolie Brise* in Concarneau where she was working as a tunny fishing boat in 1923. He bought her for £23, sailed her to Devon, and had shipwright Sydney Wright fit her out as a yacht. Wright was later Martyr's skipper. Martyr took her to the USA for the 1926 Bermuda Race, just making it back in time for that year's Fastnet, in which she placed sixth. Under new owner Bobby Somerset, heir to the Duke of Beaufort, she won the 1929 and 1930 Fastnets. Somerset took her back to the States, with *Jolie Brise* hitting the news once again when, in 1932, she saved the crew of the blazing *Adriana* in the Bermuda Race.

In the 1930s, she cruised the Mediterranean and after World War II spent most of her years in Portugal until returning to Britain in 1977. She was part of the Exeter Maritime Museum's collection and kept in commission by Dauntsey's School as living history. Three yachts have won the Fastnet twice (*Dorade*, *Myth of Malham* and *Carina*), but only *Jolie Brise* has been thrice victorious.

LOA	56ft 0in	17.06m
LWL	54ft 1in	16.48m
Beam	15ft 9in	4.84m
Draught	10ft 2in	3.10m
Displacement	123,200lb	55,800kg
Sail area	2,400sqft	223.20m²
Designer	Alexandre Paris	
Builder	M. Paumelle, Le Havre, France	
Launched	1913	

Orion page 40

After *Creole* (ex *Vira*), *Orion* stands as the second largest surviving monument to Charles E. Nicholson's design genius. She was launched in 1910, when Nicholson's work and business were flourishing to the extent that the Gosport firm was soon to take over the J. G. Fay yard at Northam in Southampton from where many of the famous racing yachts were to go down the ways.

This 147-foot schooner was commissioned by the King of Spain, but during her build she was sold to Colonel Courtney Morgan, who named her *Sylvana*. In 1915, France's Count Jean de Polignac bought her, in what was a succession of short periods of ownership: 1919, *Banu Varilla*; 1921, the owner of *Le Matin* newspaper renamed her *Pays de France*; 1922, Captain W. P. Slade renamed her *Diane*; 1927, she passed in to Argentinian hands

and crossed the Atlantic under the name of *Vira*; and, finally, in 1930 Miguel de Pinillos of Cadiz gave her the name *Orion*.

Two further owners followed. In 1935 she was sold to Manuel Bettran Mata and after sold again to the Fregesco Company who sold her in 1967 to an Italian owner until she ended up in Malta where she spent a long time slowly deteriorating. Salvation came in the form of the Banagehi brothers of Italy who moved *Orion* to La Spezia to begin an extended period of sympathetic restoration. Her composite construction meant that the hull was surprisingly sound though the copper sheathing was removed in 1987–8 to permit the mahogany carved planking to be refastened. A new rig was made in 1978 which altered her from a gaff schooner to a staysail schooner, with a new bowsprit fitted in 1995. The deck was replaced in 1991. Below, her Edwardian elegance is especially noteworthy with walnut panelling, brass grate, open hearth and mantle and candelabra in a full width saloon which, save for the height of the deckhead, could have come from an elegant turn-of-the-century London town house. The magnificence of *Orion* is such that she should be treasured. World War I and the Depression meant that few of the grand yachts survived; those that did were subject to the ravages of time. *Orion* is one of the select band of largely original survivors.

LOA	147ft 0in	44.80m
LWL	89ft 9in	27.42m
Beam	23ft 4in	7.13m
Draught	15ft 9in	4.84m
Displacement	290,528lb	131,000kg
Sail area	12,917sqft	1,200m²
Designer	Charles E. Nicholson	
Builder	Camper & Nicholson, Gosport	
Launched	1910	

Drumbeat page 41
and Bloodhound

"*Drumbeat* is the most technically ingenious yacht to have appeared for many years," intoned the serious-minded *Yachting World* annual of 1957. "She is of the American type that is becoming familiar in British waters with broad beam, shoal draught, generous overhangs, and rig of low aspect ratio." Yet, she was in the words of one who knew her well, her sometime navigator, the late Johnny Coote, "an unrewarding bitch to sail".

Sir Max Aitken, heir to the Beaverbrook newspaper fortune founded on Britain's *Daily Express*, was her owner. A noted offshore racer of both yachts and powerboats, Sir Max Aitken relished innovation. So he went to American Raymond Hunt and his associate F. C. Williams for *Drumbeat*'s design, though Clare Lallow of Cowes was her builder. The famous British orchestral conductor Sir Malcolm Sergent presented Aitken with a piano stool as a launching gift, which he sat on whilst steering.

Nowadays *Drumbeat* looks classically conventional but she was

20 per cent beamier than British ocean racers of her day and the draught achieved by her centreboard was nine feet six inches, more than 12 inches greater than that permitted under Royal Ocean Racing Club rules. It was not the depth but rather the fact that there were two boards, flat on their adjoining faces but cambered on their outboard sides, which permitted them to be configured in an asymmetric aerofoil shape that was considered her tour de force.

In 1990, designer Ed Dubois in tandem with the Berthon Boat Co. of Lymington, Hampshire, updated *Drumbeat* for her new owner, Lord Palumbo, giving her sweeter handling characteristics and modern, reliable deck gear and rig.

Accompanying *Drumbeat* here, is *Bloodhound*, an equally famous British ocean racer reunited at the Hermes-Mumm Trophy regatta in Cowes. *Bloodhound* is a Charles E. Nicholson-designed 63-footer dating from 1936. Her original owner was American Issaac Bell but she became famous for a subsequent owner, HRH The Duke of Edinburgh who kept the yacht from 1961 to 1969. The Camper & Nicholson yard updated the yacht for Prince Philip, adding a revised rig designed by Illingworth & Primrose and opening the accommodation up by removing saloon pilot berths and installing larger settees. One change not made, however, was to replace *Bloodhound*'s tiller with a wheel, despite her previous owner, Sir Myles Wyatt, a man of no mean stature, being thrown across the cockpit when steering in a difficult seaway.

Now owned by Robert Cook, *Bloodhound* has been helmed in the Hermes-Mumm Trophy at Cowes by such luminaries as Sir Peter Blake and Harold Cudmore.

LOA	58ft 0in	17.60m
LWL	40ft 0in	12.19m
Beam	15ft 0in	4.72m
Draught	9ft 6in	2.92m
Displacement	50,624lb	22,963kg
Sail area	1,645sqft	152.80m²
Designer	Raymond Hunt & F C Williams.	
Redesign	Ed Dubois	
Builder	Clare Lallow, Cowes	
Launched	1958	

Creole pages 42–3

One of the world's great yachts *Creole* was created by Charles E. Nicholson for Mr Alex Smith Cochrane. Yet before the 214-foot three-masted schooner was launched by Camper & Nicholson in 1927, *Creole* had already been sold to Major Maurice Pope and Sir Connop Guthrie and has led a chequered existence since.

Like so many of the grand yachts of the 1920s and '30s, she saw war service. The Admiralty felled her masts and *Creole* performed anti-submarine and mine-hunting duties in Scottish waters. For five years after that she languished at Camper & Nicholson until shipping tycoon Stavros Niarchos of Greece bought her in 1951. They were happy years. Niarchos raced *Creole*, lived aboard her for extended periods and ran his empire from her stately accommodations. But once again *Creole* became unloved: Niarchos laid the vessel up in Piraeus after his wife's death. She was purchased in August 1978 by the Nyborg Sofartskole (seamanship school) and though kept in commission, she was not cherished. Her Danish owners undertook a refit in Nyborg but the installation of dormitories was at the expense of her fine joinery.

In truth, such grand yachts can only be run by fabulously wealthy owners, so vast are the sums of money they consume to keep them in commission. The glory days returned in 1983 when Maurizio Gucci, of the eponymous Italian fashion house, bought her. A three-week delivery from Nyborg to Monaco took seven, such was her run down state. But a £2 million refit in La Spezia returned all the lustre to *Creole*, a celebration tinged with tragedy when Gucci was murdered in 1995.

LOA	214ft 2in	65.30m
LWL	166ft 6in	50.80m
Beam	30ft 9in	9.40m
Draught	16ft 3in	5.00m
Displacement	1,561,280lb	708,000kg
Sail area	21,958sqft	2,040m²
Designer	Charles E. Nicholson	
Builder	Camper & Nicholson	
Launched	1927	

Id page 44

Extensive sailing in his Swan 44 left American businessman James Rice well satisfied. Even so, he harboured the wish to own a wooden yacht and one with a decent heritage. A search up and down the US east coast narrowed the selection to two and his wife counselled him to choose the smaller of the two for she must have had an inkling of the scale of the undertaking.

Id was towed from Green Point on Long Island where she had lain across to the Pilots Point marina in Westbrook, Connecticut, a yard run by Dennis Conner's one time America's Cup crew man Rives Potts. There, shipwright Hans Zimmer spent eight months replacing frames, floors and working on the furniture. A generator was installed, the standing rigging replaced, new winches installed and, in Jim Rice's words: "The end result was quite worth the effort. Id is beautiful. She turns heads wherever she goes, and is a nice sailing boat as well."

Id's attractions are such that she has been seen on what Rice calls the "antique circuit", winning awards at the Antigua Classic Yacht regatta and from the Museum of Yachting in Newport, Rhode Island, though the yacht remains well used, wintering in the Caribbean and spending summers off East Hampton on Long Island. A 61-foot yawl, she was John G. Alden's design No. 713 and built by George Lawley as Irondequoit for Thomas H. Shephard, a prominent Eastern YC yachtsman who lived on Peaches Point in Marblehead. She remained in his family until the 1960s, claiming a reasonable haul of silverware in that time, before being sold to an owner in Chicago, renamed Synergy and, later, Esbro VI, with the Mayor of Chicago among those who used her. Dick Sage then bought her, returning her to Long Island via the Great Lakes, canals and Hudson River, racing her on the east coast, Florida and in the Bermuda Race before laying her up.

Which is where James Rice came in. Id? – all his yachts have carried this name. It's part of the psyche dealing with the sources of instinctive demands. Sailing, he says, is one such primitive need.

LOA	61ft 0in	18.59m
LWL	43ft 0in	13.10m
Beam	15ft 0in	4.57m
Draught	8ft 6in	2.62m
Displacement	65,470lb	29,697kg
Sail area	1,707sqft	158m²
Designer	John G. Alden	
Builder	George Lawley & Son	
Launched	1940	

Friday Star page 45

The Royal Western YC's 1972 OSTAR – originally the Observer Singlehanded Transatlantic Race but since called the C-STAR and Europe-1 STAR as sponsors have come and gone – was reaching its zenith. Entries had jumped from 35 in the previous race four years ago to 55, ranging from a tiny 19-foot Willing Griffin to the giant three-masted schooner Vendredi Treize. The only thing they had in common was the disbelief they generated as to how their

respective skippers Briton David Blagdon and Frenchman Jean-Yves Terlain could possibly sail them alone across the Atlantic.

Both did, though Terlain's race almost ended at the start in Plymouth with the narrowest of misses with Sir Francis Chichester's Gipsy Moth IV. Terlain was second home to Newport, Rhode Island in 21 days 5 hours. The yacht raced again four years later, this time called ITT Oceanic with skipper Yvon Fauconnier, and while Vendredi Treize had started arguments about whether it was seamanlike to race such a large yacht alone, Alain Colas' 236-foot Club Mediterranée brought them to a crescendo. Any collision was not likely to leave the solo sailor as the only victim, critics argued, and by the 1980 race a 60-foot length limit was in place.

Vendredi Treize was built against the expectation of starring in a film by Claude Lelouche but failing to win the 1972 OSTAR scotched the plan. Designed by Dick Carter's associate Jim Anderson, Vendredi's three-masted rig, carrying only club-footed jibs, was a cinch to tack, but the yacht lacked power when sailing other than upwind, a problem exacerbated by a pioneering attempt at foam sandwich construction which saw her weighing 37 tons instead of the designer's 25-ton target. Neglected and trying to earn her keep as a Caribbean charter yacht, Vendredi Treize was saved from ruin by Jean-Michel Tissier, chairman of Stardust Marine. As a connoisseur of thoroughbred yachts, Tissier took a mould of Vendredi and had Scorpio Maritime build Friday Star as a spiritual successor. The rig is similar, but adds a mainsail on the after mast. Displacement is 88 tons and as a charter yacht there is every possible amenity for guests in the five double cabins.

LOA	139ft 0in	42.30m
LWL	127ft 7in	38.90m
Beam	19ft 4in	5.89m
Draught	13ft 9in	4.20m
Displacement	197,120lb	90,000kg
Sail area	4,035sqft	375m²
Designer	Marc Lombard, Jim Anderson	
Builder	Scorpio Maritime, Cherbourg	
Launched	1993	

Blue Leopard pages 46–7

Of the hundreds of yachts launched in any year, a handful achieve lasting reputations. In Blue Leopard's case it was for redefining the motor-sailing concept back in 1963. Size alone, at 111 feet, made this Jack Laurent Giles design significant, but more eye-catching was Giles' marriage of sailing and motoring characteristics in the one vessel with so little compromise in performance, much to the delight of her owners, a syndicate headed by D. W. Mollins.

Blue Leopard's ketch rig is modest, giving her a total sail area

of 3,300 square feet, but so too was her displacement at 140 tons giving a power to weight ratio (i.e. sail area: displacement) not dissimilar to the prewar J-Class racers. Nine knots upwind, thanks to her 90-foot waterline length and reaching speeds of 15 knots showed her mettle. Multi-stringer construction was the key to her lightness and the search for weight-saving saw the doghouse made from aluminium alloy with some of the cabin linings utilizing fabrics in place of timber.

And when it was time to put the power down, Blue Leopard had twin 240hp Rolls Royce diesels installed. Though her stern sections were rather fuller than you would have expected in a pure sailing vessel, to avoid squat under power, Blue Leopard is still a remarkably lithe hull. She was tank-tested in the USA.

LOA	111ft 6in	33.98m
LWL	75ft 0in	22.86m
Beam	19ft 0in	5.79m
Draught	9ft 6in	2.89m
Displacement	313,600lb	142,000kg
Sail area	3,300sqft	306m²
Designer	J. Laurent Giles	
Builder	William Osborne, Cowes	
Launched	1963	

Sumurun page 48

William Fife's sensual sheerlines and the grace he put in to the overhangs of his yachts made him popular with his clients at the turn of the century and revered by enthusiasts today. Sumurun is one of his best known designs, commissioned for Lord Sackville by his wife as a rather splendid gift. Launched on the eve of World War I, she later cruised England's south coast and was notable for her modern conveniences: an ice chest and a generator. This was the heyday of the Fife dynastic design business with William Fife III at his most prolific. A 1914 edition of Lloyd's Register of Yachts lists no fewer than 308 Fife yachts as then being in class. Sumurun was a follow-up order from the 80-foot gaff yawl, Rendezvous, whose grace and speed was widely admired.

Sumurun was ruggedly constructed from elm planking with teak topside on 6x6in oak frames. During the 1920s and '30s she was raced by Hugh Paul, famous as the owner of the big class cutter Astra, before being sold in 1933 to F. W. Shenstone who installed the yacht's first engine. The change from gaff yawl to bermudan ketch in the 1950s had a profound affect on her appearance, the design work being carried out by Douglas Philips-Birt. The tiny mizzen was replaced by a much larger spar, stepped further forward and on the keel, the rationale being that the new spar was easier to handle and more efficient upwind. All this demanded a lot of the old hull. Tacking the headsails onto the stem in place of the original bowsprit eventually pulled the stem up to an extent that it was replaced in Camden, Maine, in the late 1980s, a repair initiated by Sumurun's present owner, American Robert Towbin, who bought her in 1983 from Lord Avebury.

Her oak panelling and brass fixtures are in remarkably good order though only the saloon has remained unaltered over the years. A lot of interior work was carried out in 1986 by harpsichord builder Sean Rawnsley. Using oak, inlaid with rosewood, the after cabin and guest cabin were revamped.

LOA	93ft 9in	23.65m
LWL	68ft 0in	20.73m
Beam	16ft 6in	5.06m
Draught	13ft 5in	4.11m
Displacement	201,600lb	90,000kg
Sail area	3,500sqft	325.15m²
Designer	William Fife III	
Builder	Fife of Fairlie	
Launched	1914	

Kelpie page 49

Disenchantment with rule-makers is not the sole preserve of the modern era. At the tail end of the last century the Linear Rater Rule was not entirely popular as it tried to grapple with earlier dissatisfaction at length and sail area rules. Though they tried to produce a rated length from a formula, the main complaint against the Linear Raters is that they were too lightly built. Designers might have liked them, so might the yacht builders, but the owners took a dim view. *Kelpie* was designed by Alfred Mylne as the Solent 38-foot class, a one-design to race with the 42-foot linear raters, and the fact she survives today is testament to how Mylne would have created a yacht when unconstrained by the rule. The story goes that owners who commissioned the new class decided to do so with a dinner honouring the passing of Queen Victoria, when her body was carried from Osborne House on the Isle of the Wight to the mainland.

The owners would appear to have been a slightly louche crowd, for the first yacht was named *Heroin*, as in those days, postprandial opium-smoking was not uncommon. *Kelpie* herself, trod a blatantly illegal path when she was involved in Erskine Childers' plot to run guns into Ireland in 1922 to use against the Irish Free State government. Childers was captured and executed but the 600 carbines aboard *Kelpie* were transferred to a fishing boat off Howth that slipped away undetected. Aiding *Kelpie*'s survival as the last remaining example of her class, was the fact she survived World War II with her keel intact. Many yachtsmen were encouraged to give up their keels for the war effort and *Kelpie*'s 11 tons of lead would have made a lot of bullets.

Her current owner is Brian Keelan, originally a part owner with his friend Philip Sears before purchasing her outright. Amongst a string of previous owners were the Yealm Boat Company who, in 1970, used *Kelpie* as a sailing school yacht. Adrian Stone of Cowes redecked her in 1985–6 and Peter Nash and John Holden, from her present home port of Dartmouth, have carried out work since then to achieve her current immaculate state. She was re-rigged from a yawl back to her original gaff cutter configuration after a dismasting in 1993, though naval architect Chris Temple sensibly reduced the boom length a little.

Kelpie was the pin-up on the 1997 Round the Island Race poster, a race she has made her own, winning the Shamrock Trophy three times for line honours in the Old Gaffer class and, in 1997, winning the Jubilee Trophy too for a handicap win. A diesel inboard, electric lights, some navigation aids and gas cooker are the few concessions to modernity in what is an exceptionally original yacht. "Her first owner could step aboard today and conclude things have changed very little in 100 years," says Brian Keelan.

LOA	65ft 0in	19.80m
LWL	38ft 0in	11.58m
Beam	11ft 6in	3.53m
Draught	7ft 6in	2.31m
Displacement	45,920lb	20,800kg
Sail area	2,003sqft	186m²
Spinnaker	1,505sqft	140m²
Designer	Alfred Mylne & Co.	
Builder	J. G. Fay & Co., Northam,	
	Southampton	
Launched	1903	

Inspiration pages 50–51

You might argue that *Inspiration* was an anomaly among her peers, for here was a yacht both "short" for a maxi and fitted out like a cruiser. But years after her launch in 1985 she was still competing at the highest level while her 82-foot pure racing rivals, which were little more than empty machines for racing, have fallen by

the wayside. Who got it right? "I did," will answer German Herbert Dahm, a successful businessman in the electrical and computer fields who turned his marketing genius to yachts and made a success out of the Jongert line of cruisers. They are built in the Netherlands by the Jongert yard in Medemblick who had built Dahm a yacht to cruise around the world. The German struck an arrangement to sell Jongert's yachts and it was Dahm International's sales offices that put the fizz into the Jongert marque. Having built up their reputation with heavy centre cockpit yachts, with their distinctive galleon-widowed sterns, Dahm developed a second performance orientated product.

Herbert Dahm wanted a swifter yacht, yet one he could sail comfortably with family and friends or bring a racing crew aboard to compete at the highest level. He asked Ron Holland to design the yacht and his long time associate Peter Sijm to create the styling and interior and *Inspiration* was the result. Many of her ideas have been embodied in the six other Jongert 2200s plus larger and smaller sisterships. Two crew can sail the yacht in all weathers from the semi-enclosed wheel house, thanks to her sail handling systems. Or *Inspiration* can race with 14 crew. Despite a leather and teak interior – what other racing maxi had a sit down bar in her saloon – there were many concessions to racing. Extensive use was made of foam cores in the joinery, and serious attempts were made to keep the ends of the boat empty, which was lightly built from aluminium alloy.

Over the years *Inspiration* has competed at the Maxi Worlds, Kiel Week, Nioulargue, Atlantic Rally for Cruisers, Antigua Sailing Week, Rolex Cup in the US Virgin Islands and Newport-Bermuda races. While her old sparring partners such as *Kialoa V*, *Boomerang* and *Il Moro di Venezia* no longer race the circuit, Herbert Dahm updated *Inspiration* with a carbon fibre rig and new moulded 3DL sails for the 1997 season with the Maxi Worlds in Porto Cervo, the Copa del Rey in Palma and the Nioulargue on the itinerary.

LOA	72ft 6in	22.08m
LWL	58ft 2in	17.75m
Beam	19ft 0in	5.75m
Draught	12ft 0in	3.65m
Displacement	78,400lb	35,600kg
Sail area	2,551sqft	237m²
Designer	Ron Holland	
Builder	Jongert, Medemblick, Netherlands	
Launched	1985	

Halloween page 52

The claim of this Fife 81-footer to be the first yacht expressively commissioned, designed and built to win a particular ocean race stands up to robust examination. She was ordered from William Fife III and built at his Fairlie yard by a Colonel J. F. N. Baxendale who was miffed not to have won the first Fastnet Race in 1925. He was rewarded with a line honours victory in 3 days 19 hours 5 minutes, a time which still stands as the course was altered after that from a Cowes to a Plymouth finish, though he finished third on handicap to *Jolie Brise*.

Baxendale started with what were to become several attempts at tinkering with her rig. The original bermudan cutter rig, avant-garde at the time, was changed first to a gaff and then a yawl, but the mizzen wracked the stern badly, for *Halloween* was lightly built, requiring strengthening in later life. She spent the 1930s in Norway and as the yacht of the Royal Norwegian Yacht Club the then Prince Olaf was a frequent helmsman. With World War II looming, she was shipped to the States and by 1952 came into the beneficial ownership of Walter Wheeler. A yachtsman of distinction, she became his fourth *Cotton Blossom*, and he raced her extensively on the east coast. She was a very weatherly yacht, with mizzen, mainsail, jib, staysail and flying jib and heavier than the Alden norm she was up against.

In 1986, Walter Wheeler put *Cotton Blossom IV* up for sale.

A plan for the Classic Boat Museum in Newport to take her over fell through because of lack of funds. A benefactor financed a five-year restoration by the Museum. Her name restored, she was found by European yachtsman George Ruiz, who re-rigged her as a bermudan sloop during a refit in Barcelona.

Halloween remains remarkably original and a monument to the Fife dynasty. Below deck the original panelling is as it was in 1926. The galley and crew quarters are unchanged. A chart table installed by Wheeler has replaced Baxendale's bath tub and the owner's stateroom has been extended.

LOA	78ft 0in	23.80m
LWL	48ft 6in	14.83m
Beam	14ft 4in	4.40m
Draught	10ft 0in	3.20m
Displacement	107,520lb	48,700kg
Sail area	2,131sqft	198m²
Designer	William Fife III	
Builder	Fife of Fairlie, Scotland	
Launched	1926	

Marigold page 53

Marigold is almost a metaphor for the vast amount of Britain's yachting heritage that has been allowed to whither, rot and die. After a string of illustrious owners, she was twice saved from destruction by those who believed that she should be preserved. Why? *Marigold* is one of Charles Nicholson's earliest designs, dating from 1892 when he was aged 22, and her eventual restoration stands as one of the most authentic rebuilds of either a Victorian or an Edwardian yacht.

One of those who sought to save her was artist and wood-worker Greg Powlesland, who found her in a mud berth in Wooton Creek on the Isle of Wight in 1981, and, got her to a dilapidated boathouse in Cornwall. By 1989, the impossibility of restoration without funds appeared to sink both yacht and owner until Sotheby's mooted a sale of old British yachts. Author Sam Llewellyn wrote about the sale of *Marigold* in the *Telegraph* magazine which happened to be read by Bermuda yachtsman Glen Allan on a flight back to the island from London. His interest brought him back soon afterwards to the sale and he bought *Marigold* for five times the estimate. Powlesland was asked to finish what he had started.

Glen Allan wanted *Marigold* to be as faithful as could be to her origins and the rebuild was as fastidious as it was extensive. Virtually all of it was carried out to Lloyd's 100 A1. Much of the work was carried out by shipwright John Wooley, who had experience of other C&N yachts such as *Avel* and *Partridge*. Chris Temple produced the plans for the task. All the oak frames were grown and when sufficiently long lengths of teak could not be found at a sensible price for planking, the African hardwood *paduk* was used to replank the hull. Initially, only every other plank was removed, to maintain the hull's shape. Teak was used for a new deck however. All in all, it proved to be a two-and-a-half-year job which included making wooden patterns for many of the metal fittings and casting them anew in bronze.

The lengths Powlesland went to were extraordinary. An engine was concealed in a cupboard. When new sails were ordered they were Egyptian cotton, from Jimmy Lawrence of Brightlingsea. The rig was her original gaff cutter having been converted to a yawl in 1908 and then to a bermudan rig in the 1940s. *Marigold* was sailing again by the summer of 1994, taking part in West Country regattas and classic events at Cowes from her new home berth on the piles at Buckler's Hard. Her glory days had returned, recalling those of a 1930–32 photo album which showed David Niven, Bardie Prior-Palmer and Daphne du Maurier's husband, Boy Browning, and the Bonham-Carter family on board.

LOA	59ft 0in	17.98m
LWL	47ft 6in	14.48m
Beam	12ft 2in	3.71m
Draught	8ft 9in	2.67m
Displacement	67,200lb	30,000kg
Sail area	2,690sqft	250m²
Designer	Charles E. Nicholson	
Builder	Camper & Nicholson	
Launched	1898	

Iolaire pages 54–5

Iolaire's guardsman-red hull is a famous as her owner's floppy white sun hat and the green Heineken bottle clasped in his hand. For 40 years Don Street has sailed the Caribbean, writing cruising guides and surveying charts for the Imray series.

Street bought the 46-foot yacht from Bob Cryzter for US$3,000 in 1957 on a handshake and on the understanding that another US$1,000 would be paid for each of the next four years. Since then, *Iolaire* has criss-crossed the Caribbean but not without an escapade or two. In 1959 the anchor shackle let go and *Iolaire* was stranded on a beach. Eleven new planks, 22 new frames, new bilge stringers and a new interior were fitted within 13 weeks. Two years later, the rig was lost in the middle of the night in the Anegada Passage, but Street's crew spliced it, and re-stepped it at sea. Another rig failure came in 1965 off Dominica. Street, his four-year-old daughter and a local crew sailed the boat back to Grenada, averaging 5.5 knots under jury rig.

It seems *Iolaire* was designed and built on spec by Harris Bros in 1905 on Essex's River Colne at Rowhedge. There are no drawings, so most likely she was designed on the mould loft floor and built when demand for fishing boats was quiet. *Iolaire* was treated to a thorough rebuild in 1994 by former Camper & Nicholson joiner, Mick Jarrold, in Venezuela and originally was intended to amount to no more than a new deck and deck beams. As is the way of old yachts, the more that is revealed, the greater the job becomes. In time the entire stern was rebuilt with 700 feet of new planking put in the hull and stainless steel floors in the bilge.

Iolaire made her debut in the 1995 Antigua Classic Yacht regatta, racing once more just as she had done in her youth when she was owned by a string of British yachtsmen famous for their war service and for supporting the early days of the Royal Ocean Racing Club. Among them was R. H. Bobby Somerset who, having won two Fastnets in the famous *Jolie Brise* in 1929 and 1930, did so again with a class victory in *Iolaire* in the 1951 Fastnet before selling her to an American owner. Somerset changed the rig in 1951, from gaff cutter to bermudan cutter, when he bought the spar from German Frers Snr's *Joanne* after Camper & Nicholson's fitted her with a new-fangled aluminium mast. Street added a mizzen in 1961, salvaged from Huey Long's original *Ondine* when she was wrecked on Anegada. In all, *Iolaire* can count twelve transatlantics. But what distinguishes her in Don Street's

eye is his claim that she is the oldest yacht to have remained in continuous commission since her launch, two World Wars excepted. Published in *Yachting Monthly* and *Wooden Boat* magazines the claims were rebutted by a New Zealand yacht built by Logan Bros. She doesn't count, contends Street, maintained as she has been by the Royal New Zealand Navy since the 1950s.

LOA	46ft 0in	14.02m
LWL	35ft 0in	10.66m
Beam	10ft 6in	3.23m
Draught	7ft 3in	2.25m
Displacement	49,280lb	22,300kg
Sail area	1,000sqft	304m²
Designer	Harris Bros	
Builder	Harris Bros, Rowhedge, Essex	
Launched	1905	

Lelantina pages 56–7

Ralph St L. Peverly was a considerable Alden enthusiast. Owner of the John G. Alden-designed schooner *La Goleta*, which enjoyed a great contest with *Tally Ho* in the 1927 Fastnet Race, he followed her up with *Lelanta*, built by deVries Lentsch in the Netherlands.

Lelanta aroused the interest of the legendary Cowes-based designer, builder and sailor Uffa Fox, who enthused about Alden's Grand Banks schooner-derived style. "She gives the impression of a seaworthy and comfortable schooner, one able to face any weather that comes and yet one that can be driven at a high speed."

All these characteristics were incorporated into *Lelanta II*, some 9 feet longer on deck and with much the same layout, except for no topsail on her fore mast and an extra head below decks. The original *Lelanta* then passed through a number of owners until she was captured off Naples, Florida in the late 1970s whilst involved in drug running. Ralph Peverly soon changed the name of *Lelanta II* to *Lelantina* shortly after her launch by the German yard of Abeking & Rasmussen, who had built her from rivetted iron plating in 1937. By 1955, she was owned by Prince Bina of Siam (now Thailand), grounding badly in the Mediterranean that year, and later being owned by Alberto Mandolesi and Ed Arevian.

In recent years she has undergone a major refit with some of the teak salvaged when her decks were renewed and incorporated into the re-planned pine accommodation. *Lelantina* came heart-stoppingly close to destruction in the 1980s when she was caught in bad weather on a lee shore near Cannes. The anchor was let go and she was brought up within feet of the promenade, her transom rising and falling terrifyingly close to the sea wall. It was only when the storm abated that the crew were able to determine that the anchor had caught up on the bobstay, supporting the bowsprit, and that it was a loop of chain around a rock which had averted disaster.

LOA	83ft 10in	25.56m
LWL	54ft 0in	16.45m
Beam	16ft 8in	5.54m
Draught	9ft 6in	3.24m
Displacement	145,600lb	66,000kg
Sail area	2,355sqft	216.90m²
Designer	John G. Alden	
Builder	Abeking & Rasmussen, Germany	
Launched	1937	

Puritan page 58

The times caught up with *Puritan*. She was one of John G. Alden's most beautiful schooners of the 1920s, but thanks to the Wall Street Crash, she passed through three different owners before she ever went down the ways. The commissioning owner, a Mr Curtis, cancelled his order on the day of the Crash when

Puritan was still on the drawing board. Edward Brown took her over, but sold her on quite quickly to H. J. Bauer of California. Depression or not, he maintained her in Bristol fashion, protecting her varnished spars with canvas covers when not sailing.

The Electric Boat Company's name was made by building submarines for the US Navy but *Puritan* was the first hull they attempted with butt-welded steel plating and lapped seams, a method used later to enable submarines to withstand high pressures at depth. Alden's creativity was immense yet he was largely a self-taught designer, drawing and modelling as a child, observing the America's Cup races as a teenager and then becoming a messenger in the office of the famous Edward Burgess. Alden left to work in B. B. Crowninshield's offices in Gloucester, Maine, where he was imbued with ideas on seaworthy schooners. By his retirement in 1955, John Gale Alden had produced 900 designs plus many others for government departments. Compared with his other schooners, *Puritan* had a flatter sheer, long bow and stern overhangs, a smaller transom and greater freeboard.

Puritan sailed in South American and Caribbean waters. One owner was Mariano Prado-Sosa, son of the president of Peru, and in turn she passed to vintage yacht aficionado William Bolling of Florida before passing to Austrian owner Oscar Schmidt, who had her extensively rebuilt in England. After attending the 1980 America's Cup in Newport, *Puritan* lost her main mast coming back across the Atlantic, and for a while the wayward spar threatened the vessel, but eventually she limped safely to the Canaries and was repaired in the Mediterranean.

LOA	102ft 9in	31.36m
LWL	74ft 8in	22.79m
Beam	22ft 10in	6.73m
Draught (board up)	9ft 0in	2.74m
Displacement	271,040lb	123,000kg
Sail area	4,297sqft	399m²
Designer	J. G. Alden	
Builder	Electric Boat Company, Groton, Connecticut	
Launched	1931	

Royono page 59

Legends are a powerful force. In *Royono*'s case, this 81-foot Alden yawl is forever linked with Marilyn Monroe even though there is no record of her having been aboard the yacht when she was owned by the US Naval Academy at Annapolis. It was as a Senator that John F. Kennedy first became acquainted with *Royono*, and on becoming President in 1960 he continued to sail the yacht, often with his key advisors – an informal sailing summit.

Royono's history is more colourful than a tenuous link with Hollywood and the White House for there was a genuine scandal when the yacht fell into questionable interests and was arrested in 1975 weighed down with marijuana. Towed in disgrace to Florida she was sold for a song in 1976, though her US$25,000 purchase price was too much for her young owners, Geoffrey Gibson & Mike Davies who struggled for three years to halt *Royono*'s fall from grace. It was then that Philip Bommer found *Royono* in Charlotte Amalie in the US Virgin Islands. The German industrial giant Siemens had bought the hearing aid company founded by his father so Bommer had the wherewithal to buy *Royono* and set about a labour of love. He had already restored the three-masted schooner *Shenandoah*, previously owned by Baron Bich, and knew "money no object" was the only way to tackle *Royono*.

Her steel frames and bronze fastenings had done an excellent job of destroying themselves as well as the timber around the fastenings, thanks to galvanic action. The exhaustive replacements included most of the hull and teak deck, new spars made in Tortola and rigged by Harry Spencer of Cowes, the deck houses, bulkheads and skylights replaced and much more besides. What could be saved was, such as the leaded glass cabinets in the saloon, and all replacements were kept faithful to John G. Alden's Design 623, built by the Herreshoff Manufacturing Co in 1936 for the princely sum of US$43,136. Launched as *Mandoo II*, she was a significant Alden yacht, commissioned by D. Spencer Berger to replace his previous Alden schooner. She is among Alden's most lithesome designs, her long sweeping counter part necessary to provide a sheeting base for the mizzen. A short bowsprit was a later addition because the mizzen made the helm a little hard-mouthed.

Her debut in the 1936 Bermuda was disappointing. A failed stemhead fitting saw her lose a forestay. But from 1938 she contested every Bermuda Race until 1965, winning in 1952. After Berger's ownership and either side of the US Naval Academy's custodianship, the yacht, now renamed *Royono*, had a string of owners, Philip Bommer being the seventh. 1989 saw *Royono* line up against an old Bermuda race adversary, *Ticonderoga* at La Nioulargue. In the light winds, *Royono* simply sailed away.

LOA	81ft in	24.80m
LWL	50ft 10in	15.50m
Beam	15ft 10in	4.77m
Draught	9ft 0in	2.74m
Displacement	89,600lb	40,600kg
Sail area	3,530sqft	327m²
Designer	John G. Alden	
Builder	Herreshoff Manufacturing Co, Bristol, Rhode Island	
Launched	1936	

Theta Volantis pages 60–61
and Sensation

American designer Steve Dashew tried a new twist to the formula for a long-distance cruising yacht. His line of Sundeer designs date back to the late 1970s and are aimed at easy handling by small crews, many of whom couples cruising round the world.

Theta Volantis is a Sundeer 64. Dashew gave the boat length for high speed potential. Her short ends mean that overall length of 64 feet 11 inches translates into a 64 feet 0 inches length on the waterline. Beam is moderate, or narrow, even to an eye used to the modern full volume hulls, but enables the hull lines to remain in symmetry as the yacht heels. This reduces the need for adjusting the sail plain to wind speed changes. But as this can never be avoided, the Sundeer 64 has a two-masted schooner rig, breaking down the sail plain into manageable units, each of which can be reefed by one person. Despite the narrow beam, stability is generated by a lead keel, giving a high ballast ratio. A neat trick has been to place the water tanks outboard on the hull side, so that if only the windward tank is full, some extra righting moment can be gained for "free". This is especially true as there are rain water collecting ducts to fill both tanks.

There are many standard features which appeal to live-aboard couples: numerous hatches, ports and windows; electric fans; extra thick insulation to fridge and freezer; generous water and fuel

tankage and an enormous battery bank which is sufficient to allow a Sundeer to sit at anchor for ten days, in silence mode, with lights, refrigeration and invertor still running. *Theta Volantis'* owners plan their circumnavigation and can take heart that 240-mile days are well within their reach. The first Sundeer made an October crossing from Newport, Rhode Island to Horta in the Azores in ten days, and then set a 12-day 21-hour record for the Atlantic Rally for Cruisers for the Canaries–St Lucia passage.

LOA	64ft 11in	19.54m
LWL	64ft 0in	19.50m
Beam	15ft 1in	4.62m
Draught	6ft 7in	2.04m
Displacement	48,800lb	22,135kg
Sail area	1,776sqft	165m²
Designer	Dashew Offshore	
Builder	Tillotson-Pearson International, Warren, Rhode Island	
Launched	1995	

Alejandra pages 62–3

The 90-foot *Whitefin* made an impact on her launch in 1979, and interest in newly built, classically styled yachts has been burgeoning since. *Alejandra* was commissioned from Maine-designer Bruce King by *Whitefin's* owner who wanted a substantially longer (135-foot) and sleeker vessel. Once again King has created a yacht that stands out from her peers for there are few yachts so long, so lithe and so graceful. Like *Whitefin*, *Alejandra* looked to all intents and purposes a wooden yacht, so her Spanish builders, Mefasa, recessed the waist lines and used a special aluminium extrusion for the cove line. From the intricate transom carving to her teak-clad cockpits, coamings, decks and houses, there is nothing to betray *Alejandra's* aluminium construction. For Mefasa, located at Aviles in north-western Spain, this was a big jump up from previous yachts such as the racing maxis *Kialoa V* but the quality is exemplary.

On the water, first impressions are that *Alejandra* has an "*Endeavour*-type" hull. It's not a very sophisticated critique but the clues are there: swooping sheerline, low freeboard, overhangs that seem to go on forever and a deck notably free of superstructure. King was careful to create enough deck structures to provide ample light, access and ventilation, the latter without having to resort to an army of Dorade ventilators. The rig is impressive too, allowing the crew to pile sail on to the ketch sail plan. A wing-letted keel keeps draught relatively modest for a yacht this long without resorting to a centreboard or similar device. The keel was computer modelled by Aerohydro Inc. of Southwestern Harbor, Maine, and *Alejandra's* hull tested with the keel in Webb Institute tank. In particular, King was seeking excellent upwind performance and a centre of lateral resistance which did not move markedly as the yacht heeled. This was crucial due to the helm loadings generated by such a powerful yacht and *Alejandra* remains easy to control with just direct mechanical steering.

Below, she is a haven of mahogany panelling, entered by a circular staircase and in the traditional style, her saloon's focal point is a fireplace. Just as on deck, where the wooden wheel, bronze binnacle and boom gallows suggest *Alejandra* is a wooden yacht, so does the planked and framed deckhead below. The rich red Cuban mahogany panels are solid, but the white painted ones are mostly Nomex-cored to reduce weight.

LOA	135ft 0in	41.20m
LWL	100ft 0in	30.50m
Beam	26ft 4in	8.00m
Draught	12ft 6in	3.85m
Displacement	380,800lb	173,000kg
Sail area	7,700sqft	716m²
Designer	Bruce King	
Builder	Mefasa, Austurias, Spain	
Launched	1993	

White Eagle page 64

A rare bird this, built in 1988 when the Berlin Wall was still standing. The commissioning owner took a brave step in not only having *White Eagle* constructed in the Polish Gdansk Yacht Yard, but in choosing a local designer as well.

Juliusz Strawinski had spent six years in the Yacht Yard, and another six in the technical office of the Polish Sailing Association before setting up his own design studio in which he specialized in 10–15-metre yachts for amateur building. The 36-metre *White Eagle* was a project of a different magnitude.

The Gdansk Yacht Yard were well versed with such a large vessel, having just completed 35-metre sail training barquentine *Zew* but just before *White Eagle's* plates were cut the Communist regime fell and the task of turning Poland's industry, 95 per cent of which was under state control, into private enterprises started. Janusz Zawadowicz became the yard's general manager and main shareholder. The effect was that *White Eagle* took three years to build, the first superyacht to come from a post-Communist country. A budget cap meant that she was fitted out to a modest standard but since her launch for the 1992 season, she has sailed 40,000 miles in chartering in the Mediterranean and the Caribbean. Her strength was proven when *White Eagle* was the only yacht left in St Marten intact and with her masts standing after Hurricaine Louis swept all before it. The worst damage was hull denting and a stove-in bulwark. She was sold to a Canadian owner who renamed her *Caledonia*.

LOA	119ft 0in	36.30m
LWL	74ft 8in	22.80m
Beam	24ft 4in	7.40m
Draught (board up)	8.00ft	2.45m
(board down)	22ft 11in	7.00m
Displacement	257,600lb	117,000kg
Sail area	4,736sqft	440m²
Designer	Juliusz Strawinski	
Builder	Gdansk Yacht Yard, Poland	
Launched	1992	

Lord Jim page 65

Launched as *Meridian* in 1936, *Lord Jim* was the product of two of America's greatest names in yachting: designer John G. Alden and builder Lawley & Sons of Neponset, Massachusetts.

A two-masted gaff schooner, she was one of three Alden-designed *Lord Jims* created for different owners, bonded by the Joseph Conrad fictional character. An earlier, smaller *Lord Jim* was lost on the Canimb Rock when making the passage from Boston to Mystic in Connecticut and her owner, E. Ross Anderson, later owned the larger *Lord Jim* pictured here. Anderson, commodore

of the Boston Yacht Club and part of the syndicate owning the Ted Hood-designed 12-metre *Neffertiti*, bought her from John McNamara, transferring the *Lord Jim* name to compensate for the loss of her predecessor. Before then, she had had an assortment of names: *Genie*, *Meridian*, *Shoal Water* and *Blue Water*.

Anderson had an express purpose in mind in buying *Lord Jim*: to try and beat Paul Hammond's staysail-rigged schooner, *Nina* designed by Edward Burgess. She was built for the 1928 Transatlantic race which she won, as did she the Fastnet Race that year when Sherman Hoyt skippered her. No beauty, *Nina* was powerful for her rating and carried on winning races right into the 1960s but by fitting a 12-metre spar as *Lord Jim*'s foremast and finding favourable light winds, Anderson was able to finally beat *Nina* in the 1965 Marblehead-Halifax race.

Jolyon Byerley of Antigua bought *Lord Jim* in 1966, striking a gentlemanly deal with Ross Anderson, in which as flagship of the Nicholson charter fleet, repayment of her purchase price was spread over five years from the income she brought in. She remained a famous and much loved sight plying the Caribbean waters until Jolyon Byerley sold her to an American, Denny Warner. She later got into a spot of bother on the Montezuma shoal, nothing compared to a more recent happening when, in the hands of a German/American cinematographer, she was impounded by New Zealand authorities during a leisurely round-the-world cruise. Somehow, she flew the coop and wherever she is now, this venerable yacht is not likely still to be named *Lord Jim*.

LOA	74ft 0in	22.55m
LWL	54ft 0in	16.45m
Beam	16ft 5in	5.02m
Draught	10ft 0in	3.04m
Displacement	77,800lb	35,290kg
Sail area	2,790sqft	259m²
Designer	John G. Alden	
Builder	Lawley & Sons, Neponset, Massachusetts	
Launched	1936	

Thendara pages 66–7
and *Zaca a te Moana*

Why should a leading 6-metre helmsman chose to commission a gaff-rigged ketch in the face of the established upwind prowess of the bermudan rig? That's just what Sir Arthur Young, member of Parliament for Glasgow West Central, did in 1937 when he ordered a gaff ketch with a 105-foot deck from Alfred Mylne.

The bermudan mainsail, matched to a cutter foretriangle was well accepted after its introduction in the 1920s, as offering superior windward ability to the four-cornered gaff mainsail and with little or no disadvantage in downwind speed. She won four firsts and seconds at the Torbay Royal Regatta in her 1937 debut season. Even now, after her extensive refit by Southampton Yacht Services, *Thendara* remains a witch to windward. She was built at the Scottish yard of Alexander Stephen & Son to high standards. The scarcity of both fine timber and time-served shipwrights which were a feature of post World War I boat-building had passed yet the quality of *Thendara*'s original build was top drawer. Composite construction was used: Dalzo rust-resisting steel frames and a teak keel, deadwoods and planking.

She was commandeered for barrage balloon duty in World War II but Sir Arthur Young put her back in commission directly afterwards, dying on board of a heart attack whilst savouring a sun-downer at anchor off Benodet. In the 1950s, *Thendara* passed into Continental ownership. Her stripped down hull was brought by ship from Italy along with two containers of original gear and fittings, whereupon she was sold to another European gentleman.

With little more than a few cabin doors from her original interior, SYS recreated the yacht with help from Boswell Designs

and old photos and a few drawings from the original builder and designer, all coordinated by broker Mike Horsley. Spencer of Cowes built the rig. The scale of such projects often rivals a new build, and is often more complex. One small example: the rig alone has 175 of Spencer's wooden blocks, each with the yacht's logo. Relaunched after her 1993–4 rebuild, *Thendara* was actively campaigned. She cruises with an owner's party of six, a crew of seven, the latter increased for racing.

LOA	120ft 4in	36.50m
LWL	73ft 11in	22.25m
Beam	20ft 0in	6.09m
Draught	12ft 2in	3.71m
Displacement	275,520lb	125,000kg
Sail area	6,000sqft	558m²
Designer	Alfred Mylne & Co	
Builder	Alexander Stephen & Sons, Linthouse, Scotland	
Launched	1937	

Hygie pages 68–9

Hygie was built for a life member of the prestigious Yacht Club de France, Adrien Verliac of St Malo, by the well-known Le Havre yard of Ebel Le Marchand, who kept busy constructing power boats as well as yachts. In her early years she was raced, joining the 1935 Fastnet with 17 starters: 13 British, three French and one American. *Hygie* was the sole schooner designed by the relatively unknown Frenchman Severy.

She enjoyed a second life when Betrand Danglade, owner of a chandlery on the Ile de Rez, opposite La Rochelle, carried out a total rebuilding operation. Modern equipment such as a water-maker and large diesel engine were installed as well as hydraulic winches to tame her schooner rig. Her accommodations were rearranged to provide a surprisingly high number of cabins from the skipper's right afte, with its own chart table, to a pair of double guest cabins abaft and forward of the saloon with a two-berth crew quarters right forward. Bertrand Danglade proudly showed off the fruits of his labours when *Hygie* took part in the La Nioulargue from 1988 to 1994, and again in 1996.

LOA	72ft 11in	22.25m
LWL	52ft 5in	16.20m
Beam	15ft 8in	4.10m
Draught	9ft 8in	3.00m
Displacement	134,400lb	60,900kg
Sail area	2,228sqft	207m²
Designer	Severy	
Builder	Le Marchand, Le Havre, France	
Launched	1930	

Tigris pages 70–71

An appropriate name for the sole surviving member of the Clyde 20-Ton One-Design class, though, to be fair, only six of these Victorian yachts were built. The class originated when a group of owners from the Clyde asked Alfred Mylne to design a boat expressly for them, unhappy as they were with English Yacht Racing Association rules at the time.

Mylne's plans were accepted and the first five boats were commissioned from R. MacAllister & Son of Dumbarton. *Avalon*, *Noyra*, the wonderfully named *Snarleyow*, *Tigris* and *Vagrant* were started in 1898 and were ready for the 1899 season. They were some 65 feet long with the bowsprit, or 52 feet on deck, and 35 feet on the waterline. The mainsail boom was longer than the waterline as 900 square foot of canvas was crammed on the gaff mainsail with a further 225 square foot on the jackyard topsail. The Clyde 20-Ton One-Designs managed a full 38 races in their first season, including venturing across the North Channel to regattas in Belfast Lough and further south in Dublin Bay and

for their second season they were joined by a sixth boat, *Rosemary*. Registered originally in Glasgow, *Tigris* spent time in Norway before coming back to the Clyde in 1919, when an engine was installed. Her rig was changed in 1934 to what had become the norm by then, the bermudan cutter, and in the 1950s she was a regular sight in the Solent. Her current owner treated *Tigris* to a major refit in Bristol in 1991–2, rerigging her with her original sail plan and deck layout, and sailing her on the south coast in a manner which does her Victorian heritage proud.

LOA	65ft 0in	19.88m
LWL	35ft 0in	10.68m
Beam	11ft 0in	3.35m
Draught	8ft 0in	2.43m
Displacement	47,040lb	21,200kg
Sail area	1,700sqft	157.90m²
Designer	Alfred Mylne & Co	
Builder	R. MacAllister & Son, Dunbarton	
Launched	1899	

Whitehawk pages 72–3

When she was launched in 1979, *Whitehawk* was the largest wooden sailing yacht in the USA since the 1930s, which was rather appropriate given that she owed her look to L. Francis Herreshoff's famous *Ticonderoga* and that she was built in Maine by O. Lie Nielsen, who had been *Ti*'s skipper many years previously.

Carrying twice the sail area of the maxis of the day, such as *Kialoa IV* and *Condor*, a lot of work was done on the deck gear, nearly all of it custom made, which meant a laborious process of design, drawing, pattern-making and casting. Even then, many of the original bronze castings for the goosenecks and the sheet cars had to be made again in stronger nickel aluminium bronze and stainless steel once the loads on her were better understood.

Whitehawk was three years in the making at Lee's Boat Shop in Rockland, built from triple diagonal cedar strips over a mahogany planked hull using the WEST epoxy technique. Skin thickness was 2¹/₂ in, but here again, everything about the yacht was ground-breaking. Even the ropes had to be especially manufactured because none existed which were large enough. Likewise the winches, and indeed, many items now taken for granted in the burgeoning large yacht market. The three-year build time proved too long for real estate developer Phil Long, whose boldness was to order the yacht. He asked another Californian, Bruce King, to design her, and despite the *Ticonderoga* appearance above the waterline, she had a fast, fin and skeg underbody below. King, famous for production yachts such as the Ericson 37 amongst others, started with *Whitehawk* a whole new genre of traditionally styled, high performance yachts. Thomas Zetknow of Palm Beach took over as *Whitehawk*'s owner.

Scaling up one design into another just does not work and whilst *Whitehawk* at 92 feet on the waterline is some 25 per cent longer than *Ticonderoga*, she displaces a whole 30,000 pounds

less than a straight progression of *Ti*'s displacement. As it was, *Whitehawk* was lauded in her own right: handsome, fast and progenitor of a new generation of large yachts.

LOA	105ft 0in	19.88m
LWL	92ft 0in	10.68m
Beam	20ft 6in	3.35m
Draught	7ft 5in	2.43m
(c'board down)	16ft 10in	4.90m
Displacement	170,00lb	77,112kg
Sail area	4,484sqft	416m²
Designer	Bruce King Yacht Design	
Builder	Lee's Boat Shop, Rockland, Maine	
Launched	1979	

Warrior page 74

The strong winds off South Africa's tip means that Cape Town has long produced good sailors as well as the designers and builders to create yachts to cope with conditions there. Alexander Simonis founded his design office there in the mid-1980s and by 1997 had design No. 100 on the drawing board.

Warrior is design No. 74, one of a line of light displacement, low wetted surface, beamy and high stability designs which started with the well-travelled *Broomstick*. She was pitched towards long distance blue water sailing and skipper Rick Nankin took her to second overall in the 1996 Cape–Rio race. Tackling such deep ocean races led Simonis to put a proper bow angle on *Warrior*, eschewing the plumb stems common to many modern IMS yachts to help keep the decks dry at high speed. There is practical benefit in that there is a reduced chance of the forefoot getting in the way whilst anchoring, which owner Phil Gutsche of Port Elizabeth does a fair amount of since *Warrior* is a true dual-purpose yacht. Concessions to cruising short-handed include winches that can be hydraulically powered. This helps handle the big headsails of the masthead rig, chosen over a fractional rig to both boost light air speed when racing and provide an easy way to manage mainsail for cruising. Simonis has given the boat the option to convert to fractional rig at a later stage. The deck layout splits the cockpit into three areas, the middle one is fitted with grinders for racing, whilst in cruising mode guests can sit in the seats there, while the winches become hydraulically powered and leave the area entirely free of sail controls. The grinders can be removed completely or left in place to form legs for a cockpit table.

Similarly below, the port aft section forms roomy and private accomodation for the owner, complete with its own head and shower. The saloon is multifunctional. Upper bunks can be used for racing or lowered to form back rests for the settees, in front of which removable tables can be installed.

LOA	60ft 0in	18,283m
LWL	51ft 5in	15.71m
Beam	17ft 7in	5.38m
Draught	1ft 2in	3.15m
Displacement	32,000lb	14,557kg
Sail area	1,920sqft	178m²
Designer	Alexander Simonis	
Builder	Robertson & Caine, Cape Town	
Launched	1991	

Encore page 76

When Jim Dolan wanted a more sporty yacht than his Swan 57 *Bravo*, he plumped for a Sparkman & Stephens-designed custom race boat built by Derecktor, near New York.

Painted in the same midnight blue as the other Dolan family yachts, *Bravo* and the 83-foot maxi *Sagamore*, *Encore* has competed in Antigua Sailing Week every year since her 1989 launch. In 1996, she clocked up five firsts in her class: Cruising Canvas (Non-spinnaker). She remained undefeated in that year and 1997, and is a widely travelled yacht. She has competed in the Bermuda Race three times, placing second in Class A in 1990. In 1993, she raced across the Atlantic in the event organized by the Storm Trysail Club in the USA and Britain's Royal Ocean Racing Club, going on to participate in the RORC's Channel and Fastnet Races as well as Cowes Week. She placed second in the Channel Race, something that *Sagamore* managed to do four years later in 1997. Often mistaken for a Swan for her unmistakable S&S looks, *Encore* is a fully fitted cruiser-racer. She has a full teak interior, though much of the joinery is cored for lightness while the state-rooms forward of the mast can be dismantled and removed completely for racing.

LOA	73ft 0in	22.25m
LWL	58ft 0in	17.67m
Beam	18ft 5in	5.65m
Draught	12ft 5in	3.81m
Displacement	84,000lb	38,102kg
Sail area	2,142sqft	198.90m²
Designer	Sparkman & Stephens	
Builder	Derecktor, Mamaroneck, New York	
Launched	1989	

Wallygator page 77

Cast convention aside seems to be the watchword of Luca Bassani, a noted Italian sailor and helmsman of the 6-metre *Nivola*, who created Wally Yachts to bring unconventional yachts to the market. *Wallygator* is the name of the Bassani family cruising boats, picked to make the youngest member of the family associate big, intimidating yachts with a fun and friendly cartoon character. English speakers and friends tried to persuade Lucca Bassani that 'wally' might have unfortunate connotations but he was undaunted. True to the tenets of successful marketing, Bassani has created a trademark which is not forgotten.

That is important because Wally Yachts are a "virtual shipyard", responsible for commissioning, financing and managing the design and construction of custom yachts whose actual creation is contracted out. For the first *Wallygator*, a 106-foot Luca Brenta-designed ketch, the subcontractor was Concordia Yachts in the USA.

Behind the name, have been a series of exceptionally clever yachts. Luca Bassani says that it was back in 1988, cruising on a Baltic 55, that the outline for Wally Yachts took form. "I said to myself, why can't cruising yachts be like racing boats: they are faster, they have more volume?" Rapid passage-making and fast day sailing are a given. It is the avant-garde ideas which catch the eye. Take the power and propulsion system. Recognizing that many functions on a superyacht are hydraulic powered, Wally discarded the idea of a main engine driving the yacht through a conventional propeller shaft. Instead two small Yanmar engines are fitted, driving hydraulic pumps. Besides the usual functions of handling the bathing platform and powering the sail controls, the pumps also drive two retractable four-bladed thrusters – one in the bow and one amidships. They turn such a large yacht into a very wieldly beast, able to slip out of her berth sideways. Under power, one thruster gives 10 knots boatspeed, two give 12 knots, whilst under sail, the gain from a completely flush underbody is said to be a knot. Invisible anchoring is another trick up *Wallygator*'s sleeve. A 250-pound anchor is stowed in a cassette and deployed through doors which open and close like an aircraft's landing gear. There is more hidden from view. The yacht's 11 feet 10 inch draught can be increased to 16 feet 11 inches to give real bite to her upwind performance by a dagger board which is housed entirely in the keel, sliding out through the bulb: intrusion into the accommodation is non-existent.

Luca Bassani has followed up this 105-foot ketch with similarly sized and smaller yachts from Luca Brenta and German Frers. Watch for a Wally: you are sure to be in for a pleasant surprise.

LOA	105ft 0in	32.04m
LWL	90ft 9in	27.93m
Beam	26ft 0in	8.00m
Draught	11ft 10in	3.60m
(d'board down)	16ft 11in	5.16m
Displacement	132,160lb	60,300kg
Sail area	5,704sqft	530m²
Designer	Luca Brenta	
Builder	Concordia Custom Yachts, USA	
Launched	1984	

Alitea page 78

The original Swan 65 design from Sparkman & Stephens was one of the best yachts stemming from the 20-year partnership between the famous New York design office of Sparkman & Stephens and the Finnish builders, Nautor. S&S designed the very first Swan, a 36, and 11 subsequent models representing 800 out of the first 1,000 Swans built

Some 41 Swan 65s were produced with the model staying in production an uncommonly long time from 1972 to 1989, which required very careful husbandry of the mould tools, and was a remarkable run given that a 65-footer was considered much more of an unusually large yacht in the 1970s than it is now. The combination of an elegant sheer, a wedge deck which really suited a hull this long and a fundamental rightness about it, means the Swan 65 has not lost its ability to turn heads.

Alitea is now one of the most successful 65s racing on the Nautor Swan regatta circuit. Originally produced in both a ketch version and with a sloop rig – the first being Nick Ratcliffe's *King's Legend* which placed second in the 1977–8 Whitbread Round the World Race – *Alitea*'s is a hybrid: a ketch with the taller mainmast from the sloop version.

Owned for many years by a Gibraltar company, Quick Tide Ltd, *Alitea* enjoys her reputation as the fastest 65 in the world. Not only is she powerful, but has good speed for her rating, always has excellent sails and often has top-flight crews. When she placed fifth amongst a 70-boat fleet in the 1996 Swan World Cup, her tactician was American Dee Smith, a familiar fixture on top grand-prix boats the world over.

LOA	64ft 5in	19.68m
LWL	47ft 0in	14.33m
Beam	16ft 3in	4.96m
Draught	9ft 6in	2.90m
Displacement	70,000lb	31,800kg
Sail area	2,224sqft	2,066m²
Designer	Sparkman & Stephens	
Builder	Nautor, Pietarsarri, Finland	
Launched	1979	

Creighton's Naturally page 79

A triple circumnavigator, *Creighton's* began life as George Stead's *Ocean Greyhound*, built in 1980 by the Southern Ocean Shipyard in Poole and was raced as *FCF Challenger* in the 1981–2 Whitbread race by Britain's Les Williams. She had rarely shone in the race when on the final leg, her big fractionally-rigged mainmast collapsed between the Azores and home.

The colourful Williams kept going for a while after the Whitbread, re-rigging the boat with a heavy, bulletproof masthead rig, still carrying the colours of FCF – First Co-Operative Finance. But things turned sour and the boat languished in Moody's yard on the River Hamble at Swanwick. Which is where Tony Allen, John Chittenden and Malcolm McEwan came in. Variously a marine lawyer, Royal Yachting Association cruising secretary and RYA instructor, they managed to buy the boat for a song – £50,000 – and set about a campaign to race her in the 1989–90 Whitbread, the last race to have a division for cruising yachts. With little money, a huge bank loan, they took the boat to Hull where she gained huge support and a refit was carried out, ready for an amateur crew to race around the world having bought their berths. It was a concept which Chay Blyth turned into his hugely successful British Steel and BT Global Challenges.

Richard Collard became more of a benefactor when his company's name went on the boat – Creighton's, one of the Body Shop's main suppliers – and the fact that *Creighton's* was at the back of the fleet only made his support more unwavering. All the more so when tragedy struck in the Southern Ocean on Leg 2, when bad seas broached the boat twice on 12 November 1989. Two crew went over the side as the damage was being cleared away. Both were recovered, Bart van den Dwey after 45 minutes and who was resuscitated, and 15 minutes later, Tony Phillips, who could not be. He was buried at sea. The concept of pay-berths was well established and the Allen/Chittenden/McEwan partnership took the boat around again, more slowly this time and visiting remote places such as Ascension Island, the Kerguelen Islands, Ushuaia and Puerto Williams in Patagonia and Jan Meyen Island. A promotion with the *Financial Times* newspaper kept bookings for several years before *Creighton's Naturally* was sold to her current owner Stuart Bowen-Davies.

LOA	80ft 0in	24.34m
LWL	70ft 0in	21.33m
Beam	20ft 6in	6.27m
Draught	12ft 6in	3.84m
Displacement	75,936lb	34,500kg
Sail area	3,400sqft	320m²
Designer	David Alan-Williams/Doug Peterson	
Builder	Southern Ocean Shipyard, Poole, Dorset	
Launched	1979	

Golden Aura page 80

In a former life, *Golden Aura* was a drug runner. The ability to come and go by sea, clad in a veneer of innocence, has meant that yachts have been used for illegal purposes. In *Golden Aura's* case it happened when the original Italian owner of this Swan 55 sold her to the USA, which is how she was later seized by the US Customs.

For eight years she languished ashore until she was sold in a government auction and completely refurbished. On the market again, Briton Brian Bailey saw her in Boston and bought the yacht using the proceeds from his company being the target of a hostile takeover by an American corporation. She arrived back in the UK via stops in Bermuda and St Maarten.

Under Brian Bailey's ownership, *Golden Aura* has made two crossings of the Atlantic though her return to St Maarten coincided with Hurricane Louis. He is proud of the yacht's sail number – GBR 5502T – denoting she is the second of the 16 Swan 55s built between 1970 and 1974. She is one of the old-style Sparkman & Stephens-designed Swans and that suits Brian Bailey down to the ground. "It's been a lifetime ambition to own a Swan and one of the S&S types at that," he explained. "I fell in love with her when I saw *Golden Aura* and I am still in love."

LOA	54ft 6in	16.65m
LWL	38ft 4in	11.73m
Beam	14ft 2in	4.33m
Draught	8ft 5in	2.60m
Displacement	45,600lb	20,700kg
Sail area	1,344sqft	124.80m²
Designer	Sparkman & Stephens	
Builder	Nautor, Pietarsaari, Finland	
Launched	1970	

Fire Dancer page 81

Max Aitken was the great patron of the London Boat Show during the 1960s and '70s introducing the Boat of the Show award in 1965. Lunch was a vital part of the deliberations and the small group of journalists and technical advisers in the judging panel declared the Kim Holman-designed *Fire Dancer* the first winner.

Today we would routinely refer to her as a 41-footer, but the *Yachting World* report of the show recorded her as a 30-foot waterline auxiliary sloop. "*Fire Dancer* is a lovely example of traditional wooden boat building at its very best," *Yachting World* reported. "A type of construction with is steadily being squeezed out of the yachting scene by the introduction of reinforced glass fibre and by the lack of suitably skilled craftsmen."

Interestingly, the magazine hailed the glassfibre *Liz of Lymington* as one of the show's most interesting boats, another Holman design. C. R. "Kim" Holman was then senior partner in the Holman & Pye office which still prospers and *Fire Dancer* was their Design No. 65, built by A. H. Moody at Swanwick on the River Hamble for D. S. Cottell, who was then a rear-commodore of the Royal Southern YC. A Bursledon resident, he would have been able to watch his yacht take shape just across the river. She was a development of the Holman & Pye designed *Whirlaway*, with a 3-inch greater draught and modified rudder shape which required an altered transom profile. As a keen offshore racer – D. S. Cottell was one of Ron Amey's crew aboard *Noryema IV* in the 1966 Onion Patch Series in New York and Bermuda – *Fire Dancer* was raced extensively. She was sold to R. M. Bowker in 1968.

LOA	41ft 7in	12.71m
LWL	30ft 2in	9.20m
Beam	10ft 10in	3.07m
Draught	6ft 9in	2.10m
Displacement	24,080lb	10,900kg
Sail area	720sqft	66.80m²
Designer	Holman & Pye	
Builder	A. H. Moody & Son, Swanwick	
Launched	1965	

Anse Chastenet pages 82–3

For all the art and, increasingly science, involved in yacht design, some boats are just right from the word go. The German Frers-designed Swan 46 is one such yacht, a pleasure to sail, competitive under many systems and such a popular model that it remains in production more than 15 years after it was introduced. With 109 built at the last count, it is the best-selling yacht ever built by Nautor of Finland and by a considerable margin.

Anse Chastenet was the 13th Swan 46 produced and, in the hands of Norman Brick, one of the most vigorously campaigned. Here she is beating out through the Needles Channel at the start of the 1991 Fastnet Race; having slipped through the tidal gate at Portland Bill she was miles ahead of her rivals until she got bogged down in light winds beyond Land's End.

Norman Brick bought *Anse Chastenet* in 1983 and she has crossed the Atlantic every year since then, wintering in the Caribbean on her mooring in Chastenet Bay, St Lucia, where her owner built two houses, and then spending the summer in the US, UK or Mediterranean. *Anse Chastenet* has had two skippers in that time and one of them, Jon Smallridge, brought her back across the Atlantic on his own. In that time, there has not been an event in Antigua, Martinique, Barbados, St Maarten or St Lucia that *Anse Chastenet* has not won and not for nothing is Norman Brick an unashamed admirer of German Frers' work. He once said to the late Rod Stephens of Sparkman & Stephens, designers of Swans in the 1960s and '70s: "German must have learnt a lot during his time in the S&S office." "On the contrary," Stephens replied, "we learnt a lot from him."

LOA	47ft 1in	14.36m
LWL	37ft 8in	11.55m
Beam	14ft 4in	4.41m
Draught	8ft 2in	2.50m
Displacement	31,300lb	14,200kg
Sail area	1,142sqft	106.50m²
Designer	German Frers	
Builder	Nautor, Pietarsaari, Finland	
Launched	1985	

Splendid page 84

After a string of Standfast yachts from Breskens builder and designer Frans Maas, the owner of *Splendid* selected one of the larger yachts from Finnish builders Nautor for his first Swan. She is a Swan 68, originally launched as *Hissar* for an American owner, and the ninth of the 18 or so 68s built since 1991. She was sold to a Dutch yachtsman in 1995 who uses her primarily for cruising, enjoying all the comfort, quality and amenities Swans are famous for. She has become a regular Atlantic commuter, following the sun to the Caribbean in winter and back again to the Mediterranean in summer. St Maarten and Antibes have been her bases in recent years.

Splendid has also raced on the well-established Rolex Swan regatta circuit, taking part both in the Atlantic regatta in Newport, Rhode Island whilst she was *Hissar*, and the 1996 World Championships in Porto Cervo, Sardinia, where she placed ninth. She is one of three 68s to be fitted with a carbon fibre rig, losing her original one when a metal backstay fitting failed. The weight savings in her carbon fibre mast are transferred into a slightly lighter keel and, in keeping with Nautor's ability to customize their boats to individual tastes, she has an extended stern.

LOA	69ft 9in	21.31m
LWL	54ft 7in	16.18m
Beam	17ft 8in	5.42m
Draught	11ft 6in	3.55m
Displacement	88,200lb	40,000kg
Sail area	2,735sqft	254.10m²
Designer	German Frers	
Builder	Nautor, Pietarsaari, Finland	
Launched	1993	

Loire Atlantique page 85

Jeanneau is one of the giants of French boat-building although financial difficulties put it in the hands of its long-time rival Beneteau in the early 1990s. Largest in the Sun Fast line is the 52 of which *Loire Atlantique* is one, designed for the volume producer by Philippe Briand. The boat's speed is appreciated by those owners who use their boats for cruising and chartering, with the

builders offering a choice of a three-cabin layout with six berths or four cabins sleeping eight. The Sun Fast 52 has also proved a useful cruiser-racer. *Loire Atlantique* is a case in point, winning the Barquera regatta in 1992, placing second during the Spi Ouest regatta at La Trinité sur Mer during Easter and then coming across the Channel to England for Cowes Week 1993.

LOA	51ft 1in	15.56m
LWL	44ft 4in	13.50m
Beam	14ft 6in	4.42m
Draught	8ft 7in	2.65m
Displacement	29,120lb	13,000kg
Sail area	1,108sqft	103m²
Designer	Philippe Briand	
Builder	Jeanneau, Les Herbiers, France	
Launched	1992	

Elysia pages 86–7

For *Elysia*'s original British owner, Tony Vernon, the jump from his previous yacht, the Laurie Davidson-designed One Tonner *Canterbury*, could not have been greater. Gone was the austere emptiness of the race boat interior and in its place were full cruising amenities of his new Mystic 60 yacht.

Having comfort did not mean having to give up racing. Soon after delivery in 1990, *Elysia* competed in the Brent Walker European Cup from Brighton, England, to Porto Sherry near Cadiz, winning the Concours d'Elegance Prize. Being so near Gibraltar, the yacht made a quick foray into the Mediterranean to take part in La Nioulargue at St Tropez before heading east once more, to the Canaries and the start of the ARC (Atlantic Rally for Cruisers) from Las Palmas to St Lucia where *Elysia*'s long legs and easy gait made her sixth boat home.

Back in UK waters for the 1991 season, *Elysia* sailed in the Cork Dry Gin Round Ireland and Fastnet Races. One of the reasons Tony Vernon chose the Taiwan-built, German Frers-designed Mystic 60 was that her centre cockpit and comfortable interior made her a very good yacht for chartering and cruising and *Elysia* turned into a transatlantic commuter with winters in the Caribbean and summers in the Mediterranean. She took part in two more ARCs (again amongst the first six to finish), three Antigua Sailing Weeks, two Nioulargues and cruised all over the Mediterranean save for the Adriatic and North African coast. Her current Spanish owner keeps her in Porto Pollensa, Mallorca.

LOA	59ft 11in	18.28m
LWL	47ft 8in	14.55m
Beam	16ft 3in	4.95m
Draught	9ft 6in	2.90m
Displacement	56,336lb	25,550kg
Sail area	1,605sqft	144m²
Designer	German Frers Jr	
Builder	Ta Shing, Taiwan	
Launched	1991	

Bravo page 88

Bravo is one of three yachts in this Beken selection owned by American businessman Jim Dolan. She is very much the family yacht, a Swan 57 ketch used by Mr Dolan, his six adult children and grandchildren. With an extended family all keen on sailing, raising a crew is never a problem.

A centreboard version of the Swan 57, *Bravo* spends her summers on Long Island Sound and winters in the Caribbean and from 1995 to 1997 was the best Swan at Antigua Sailing Week. When the Dolan family decided to build a larger yacht, appropriately named *Encore*, they returned to the Sparkman & Stephens design office which had served them so well. They also decided, as a family so attached to its sailing, that *Bravo* would not be replaced, rather augmented by the 79-foot custom boat *Encore*, when she was launched in 1989. And when the Dolans decided to move up the scale from *Encore*, to the S&S-designed 83-foot grand-prix maxi *Sagamore*, both *Bravo* and *Encore* were retained in the stable. All three yachts were raced at Antigua Sailing Week 1997.

LOA	57ft 4in	17.50m
LWL	45ft 8in	13.96m
Beam	15ft 8in	4.83m
Draught (board up)	6ft 4in	1.95m
(c'board down)	10ft 2in	3.10m
Displacement	51,500lb	23,400kg
Sail area	1,580sqft	146.80m²
Designer	Sparkman & Stephens	
Builder	Nautor, Pietasaari, Finland	
Launched	1984	

Out of the Blue page 89

Light displacement boats are often linked with the US West Coast and though the "sled" style of yacht is popular there, plenty of other designers have gone down the lightweight route. Michel Joubert was a pioneer in France, with his aptly named *Subversion*, which rattled around the Royal Ocean Racing Club's races in the 1973 season. Guy Ribadeau-Dumas is another practitioner, best known for designing two 60-foot *Credit Agricole* monohulls for Philippe Jeantot which he took to victory in the first two BOC solo round the world races. *Out of the Blue* is another Ribadeau-Dumas design, built by the Pinta yard in La Rochelle in a female mould from foam-cored laminate.

The designer has used some of his BOC experience by applying water ballast to *Out of the Blue*. She carries 750 litres per side. An idea of the righting power this generates is that it is sufficient to heel the boat about 5 degrees in static trim. The performance gain is tangible. In 20 knots of true wind and under plain sail of full main and Solent jib, filling the windward tank adds more than half a knot to the speed. Gravity transfers the water when tacking. Another BOC idea, twin rudders as opposed to a single blade on the centre line, gives good control when the boat is fully powered up under spinnaker and makes *Out of the Blue* particularly suitable for steering by autopilot. Light displacement can make a yacht perform better than you'd expect for her length, and Ribadeau-Dumas has given *Out of the Blue* a big masthead rig to ensure she is not disadvantaged in low wind speeds. "In the light airs of Antigua, the boat sailed as well as the maxis," the designer reported, "and during a passage in the Bay of Biscay, she hit a speed of 22 knots." Used for chartering, *Out of the Blue* spent three years in the Caribbean taking part in the regatta circuit there. In the summer of 1997, she was used by the organizer's of the Solitaire au Figaro, a solo triangle race in the Western Approaches, as mother ship.

LOA	50ft 0in	15.24m
LWL	44ft 2in	13.45m
Beam	13ft 7in	4.20m
Draught	8ft 6in	2.60m
Displacement	17,920lb	8,100kg
Sail area	1,367sqft	127m²
Designer	Guy Ribadeau-Dumas	
Builder	Chantiers Pinta, La Rochelle, France	
Launched	1993	

Force 9 pages 90–91

Not so very long ago, *Force 9*'s owner was sipping a drink outside a Greek taverna. He'd chartered a yacht to sail the Greek islands and was thumbing through the yacht broker's advertisements in *Boat International* magazine when a pale blue Swan 65 caught his eye. The taverna's owner let him make a call to Newport Beach, California. From there, brokers Ardell faxed back the yacht's specification and inventory. A second phone call announced that the Italian yachtsman would be sending his skipper to the US to inspect in four days time. He found *Force 9* everything she was described to be and the owner travelled to California shortly afterwards and the deal was done.

The original Swan 65 from Sparkman & Stephens was one of the very best stemming from a 20-year partnership between the Finnish builder and the New York design office. Some 41 were built and the model stayed in production an uncommonly long time, from 1972 to 1989, which asked a lot of the mould tooling, and even today the head-turning looks of the Swan 65 remain unsurpassed by virtually any other glassfibre series-built yacht.

Force 9 was, appropriately, the ninth 65 to be produced but will be remembered as *ADC Accutrac* when Clare Francis become the Whitbread race's first women skipper in 1977–8. Victory by Ramon Carlin's Swan 65 *Sayula* in the first Whitbread brought three to the start line four years later. Francis' yacht was sponsored by an electronics company who thought a round the world race would be the right way to promote a new tone arm aimed at serious hi-fi buffs. *ADC Accutrac* finished fifth overall, beaten by both her sisterships, but out of the 27 starters, Francis led the only crew to remain unchanged all the way round.

Sold to the US West Coast, the yacht was cruised by her first American owner between the Mexican Riviera, Catalina and San Francisco and always kept in pristine condition. A major refit was undertaken at Marina del Rey, Los Angeles, with new decks laid, hydraulic winches and furling added, air-conditioning installed and a complete interior refurbishment, right down to hand painted Italian leather upholstery.

LOA	64ft 7in	19.68m
LWL	47ft 0in	14.33m
Beam	16ft 3in	4.96m
Draught	9ft 6in	2.90m
Displacement	70,000lb	31,800kg
Sail area	1,797sqft	166.90m²
Designer	Sparkman & Stephens	
Builder	Nautor, Pietarsaari, Finland	
Launched	1974	

Magic pages 92–3

Despite his best intentions, Pieter Vroon, couldn't help racing *Magic*, a 50-foot Frers-designed yacht which he had bought ostensibly for cruising. Offshore racing is very much in Vroon family blood with Pieter Vroon joining the Royal Ocean Racing Club back in 1959 and remaining an ardent supporter of its club races and major events, particularly the Admirals' Cup, ever since.

His long time sailing partner has been Breskens boat-builder Frans Maas, with whom he has campaigned *Tonnerre de Breskens*,

three Maas-designed Standfasts, two *Formidables* (one the former 1975 Holland-designed *Marionette* and the other a Dubois-designed 44-footer) and new in 1997, a Lutra 52 which once again bears the *Tonnerre* name.

Magic is one of two cruising yachts Pete Vroon has owned, the other being *Cashflow*, a Maas 50-footer bought in California, so the idea of bringing *Magic* back to Europe from far away overseas was not new. *Magic* was built by Queen Long in Taiwan and finished by Hamble Yacht Services near Southampton. Every year since her launch in 1992, *Magic* has raced at Cowes Week, twice winning the IMS class there outright, the biennial Cork Week in Ireland and a number of RORC races such as the North Sea Race, Cowes–St Malo, Channel and Fastnet Race.

LOA	50ft 6in	15.40m
LWL	42ft 0in	12.80m
Beam	15ft 7in	4.80m
Draught	8ft 5in	2.60m
Displacement	40,320lb	18,200kg
Sail area	1,260sqft	117m²
Designer	German Frers	
Builder	Queen Long, Kaoshiung, Taiwan	
Launched	1992	

Ayesha pages 94–5

The two 65-foot Swan types built by Nautor form neat bookends at either end of the Finnish builder's involvement in the Whitbread Round the World Race. The first 65, a Sparkman & Stephens design, was winner of the inaugural Whitbread in 1973–4 in the shape of Ramon Carlin's *Sayula* whilst the German Frers-designed 651 was the last Swan to take part in the Whitbread when *Fazer Finland* placed third in the 1985–6 event. By then, the days of the cruiser-racers were largely over. Custom built, stripped out race boats were fast becoming the norm.

Ayesha has a tenuous Whitbread link – she has one of *Fazer*'s old spinnakers. Always British owned, she was bought as the ten-year-old *Thair* in 1994 by Roger Boyland, who has had 20 years in the commercial property business in Britain and the USA, and renamed her after his niece. Since then she has been leading the life Swans exemplify best. She commutes each winter from the Solent to the Caribbean, has raced in Antigua Sailing Week and cruised as far south as St Lucia, with the Grenadines still beckoning. She has also competed in Rolex Swan regattas, photographed here at the 1995 Europeans in the Solent, being raced by Roger Boyland's family and friends. "It was always nice to get the gun for being first to finish, though the corrected time results weren't so good," he recalled.

Ayesha, sixth of the 19 651s built between 1982 and 1991, is a successful charter yacht, competing in the Round the Island race, Cowes Week, and in 1995, in the Fastnet when a group of American lawyers fulfilled an ambition to compete in one of the world's classic ocean races.

LOA	65ft 6in	19.98m
LWL	55ft 1in	16.80m
Beam	17ft 4in	5.30m
Draught	11ft 6in	3.50m
Displacement	75,000lb	34,000kg
Sail area	2,088sqft	194m²
Designer	German Frers Jr	
Builder	Nautor, Pietarsaari, Finland	
Launched	1985	

Rrose Selavy page 96

The latest *Rrose Selavy* is the first Wally Yacht. Owned by Dot. Riccardo Bonadeo, president of the North Sails in Italy, she embodied the ideas of Lucca Bassani in creating Wally Yachts: high performance, high technology, high speed boats in which no effort was spared for extreme comfort. *Wallygator* is another yacht embodying these aims.

In the space of three years she has won most of the Mediterranean's top events for IMS boats: in 1994 and 1995 she was best overall yacht at La Nioulargue in St Tropez; top yacht in the 1995 Maxi event in Porto Cervo, Sardinia; winner of the 1995 and 1997 Zegna Trophy in Portofino.

Her performance stems from a powerful design from German Frers and light Nomex-cored carbon fibre construction by Yachting Developments in Auckland, a combination which has seen this yacht fulfil her dual purposes admirably where many others have fallen short. In race mode, the crew have pedestal driven primary winches and a clean deck. In cruising mode, electricity not brawn drives the winches and just two people can sail the boat. The cockpit becomes a large social and sun-bathing area with a table which can seat up to ten for *al fresco* meals. Below, the owner's stateroom has two large beds and all amenities, a large social area and galley plus two double guest state rooms for wining, dining and winning.

LOA	665ft 7in	20.05m
LWL	53ft 8in	16.40m
Beam	17ft 1in	5.24m
Draught	11ft 6in	3.50m
Displacement	51,807lb	23,500kg
Sail area	2,160sqft	200.60m²
Designer	German Frers	
Builder	Yachting Developments, Auckland	
Launched	1994	

Wolf page 97

"Where do I go from here?" was the question Scot Geoff Howison asked himself having moved out of IOR race boats and into the Etchells 22 day-boat class. It was a similar question that Aussie Ian Bashford was asking, having built J/24s, Etchells and the J/35 and when the two men put their heads together the Bashford-Howison 41 IMS cruiser-racer was the result.

Geoff Howison had already spoken to several designers but Bashford was keen to keep the project all-Australian. Iain Murray's design office on Pittwater, north of Sydney, had already carried out extensive research into an ILC40 design, including 20 computer models and three which were run in the test tank, but the decision was made to tool up a development for production.

The hull was made wider because there would be less ballast and the freeboard increased to improve internal volume. At the same time the IMS accommodation rules came in, so a full length coachroof was added. Murray's worries about the boat being built down to weight in series production proved groundless thanks to "Basho's" clever detailing and structural internal mouldings.

Straightaway the boat proved a winner, victorious in the 1994 Sydney–Hobart race and racking up win after win after that. *Wolf* is the ninth BH41, owned by Glyn Williams of Wales, and for the 1996 season in the UK, she was campaigned by Matt Humphries and some of his crew from the 1993–4 Whitbread entrant *Dolphin & Youth*. Under CHS or IMS, *Wolf* notched up a string of top results, winning the RORC's De Guingand Bowl, St Malo and Le Havre in CHS Class 1 and being IMS winner in the Berthon Source regatta and Cowes Week.

Williams previously owned the IMX 38 *X-pro*, ironically, precisely the yacht Howison decided was too small when he began his search for a new yacht which led to his partnership with Bashford. Sadly, Bashford died of a heart attack in 1996. New investors restructured Bashford Boat-builders at Nowra in New South Wales, bought the BH41 moulds from Howison and took a copy from the follow-up BH36 tooling.

LOA	41ft 0in	12.50m
LWL	39ft 0in	11.88m
Beam	12ft 2in	3.75m
Draught	8ft 6in	2.60m
Displacement	15,4000lb	7,000kg
Sail area	1,221sqft	113.50m²
Designer	Iain Murray & Associates	
Builder	Bashford Boat-Builders, Nowra, Australia	
Launched	1996	

Vivant pages 98–9

The "stop-you-in-your-tracks" topsides finish sums up the owner's pride in *Vivant*, a 73-foot German Frers-designed yacht. She has a *faux* blue marble finish, a *trompe l'oeil* effect which comes alive when the sea reflects strong sunlight onto the hull.

Built from aluminium alloy by the French yard Chantier Naval de Bordeaux, *Vivant* is Canadian-owned and the third of a limited series built for high performance cruising with all possible comforts: ice-maker, air-conditioning, multi-standard TV and video, hard-bottomed tender and windsurfer included. The interior was designed by Olivier Lafourcade and Hervé Couedel, and includes three guest cabins for six plus another pair of double-berth cabins forward of the mast which convert to a state room.

Since her launch in 1995 she has been continuously on the move, to stay in perpetual sunshine: summer in the Mediterranean and winter in the Caribbean. The rig is a masthead cutter and Frers has created a hull that is rewarding in performance yet docile and well-mannered for comfortable passage-making.

LOA	76ft 6in	23.35m
LWL	62ft 0in	18.90m
Beam	19ft 8in	6.00m
Draught	9ft 8in	3.00m
Displacement	89,600lb	40,600kg
Sail area	2,572sqft	239m²
Designer	German Frers	
Builder	Chantier Naval de Bordeaux	
Launched	1993	

Anahita pages 100–101

When *Anahita* came to race in the 1993 Cowes Week it was her first visit to the English regatta since 1965. With her brightly varnished topsides and upper works and elegant lines, she looked like a yacht from another era.

Appearances can be deceptive however, for under the water her old full keel with the rudder hung on its trailing edge had been replaced with a modern deep fin and blade rudder configuration designed by Peter Norlin. On deck, stood a new 22-metre aluminium mast in place of the original ketch sail plan, which, unusually, had featured two glassfibre masts made by the Plym shipyard in Stockholm. This revamp was begun by her present owner, Swede Hans Drakenberg, in 1986, and a big effort from Diamond Sails of Copenhagen made *Anahita* competitive enough to take second place under the CHS in the Royal Ocean Racing Club's Channel Race plus a Class 1 win during Cowes Week.

Anahita came back to the UK in 1995, having rating optimization carried out by Hugh Welbourn. She didn't find the generally light winds of Cowes Week much to her liking but claimed a second in class in the Fastnet Race, returning to Scandinavia and winning IMS Class 1 in the Round Gotland Race, northern Europe's premier offshore race. She is now restored to full cruising standard with no further racing planned. This blossoming second racing career is far removed from her 1961 origins when noted 5.5-metre and 6-R-metre designer Arvid Laurin drew her for Olle Berger who maintained the yacht right through to 1985. After her launch, she was campaigned extensively in Scandinavian waters, including a class win in the Baltic Race, which alternates bi-annually with the Round Gotland event.

LOA	52ft 0in	15.80m
LWL	39ft 0in	11.88m
Beam	13ft 0in	3.96m
Draught	9ft 3in	2.80m
Displacement	42,560lb	19,300kg
Sail area	1,657sqft	154m²
Designer	Arvid Laurin	
Builder	Jacobsson Brothers, Sweden	
Launched	1961	

Cisne pages 102–3

A student of yacht design, even on the first day of his course, would be able to pick out *Cisne* as a design from Sparkman & Stephens in their heyday. She is a Swan 43 dating from 1969 when Nautor's production yachts in glassfibre were not so very different from a custom racer built in aluminium or timber.

S&S's Madison Avenue offices in New York was the engine room of yacht design in the 1960s and early '70s and *Cisne* displays the subtly radiused bow angle, sweeping down to the tip of the keel that was so characteristic of Olin Stephens' work of the time. There was a trim tab on the trailing edge of the keel and on deck, all manner of seamanlike details for which Rod Stephens was renowned. It was the values that such an old design embodies that attracted *Cisne*'s Dutch owner, Koert Jansen, to the Swan 43 when he bought her in 1993. "The Swan 43 is to my liking, she is rather classical and has a certain air about her. She is a little ship, 12 tons in weight, not like so many modern yachts which seem no more than dinghies!"

Cisne was bought from a German owner who had kept her in the Adriatic, and being 25 years old, she required a lot of work. Her previous owner had tackled osmosis in the glassfibre, having the gel coat and some laminate peeled off and replaced as well as swapping the engine, deck fittings and teak deck. Koert Jansen completed the overhaul with new standing rigging and many new sails. This new lease of life was amply rewarded. Koert Jansen has gathered an enthusiastic crew around him, racing first in the Netherlands in the 1993 and 1994 seasons before coming to Cowes for their first international event, the 1995 Rolex Swan European Cup. *Cisne* was fourth overall. This spurred the crew on to tackle the 1996 Rolex Swan World Cup in Port Cervo, Sardinia, where *Cisne* was 14th overall, hampered it transpired by a folding propeller which was not closing properly, but still a very respectable result in a 72-boat fleet.

LOA	42ft 9in	13.04m
LWL	31ft 0in	9.45m
Beam	11ft 7in	3.55m
Draught	7ft 2in	2.20m
Displacement	22,000lb	10,000kg
Sail area	822sqft	76.60m²
Designer	Sparkman & Stephens	
Builder	Nautor, Pietarsaari, Finland	
Launched	1969	

Windsong page 104

The Swan 57 was one of the last of Sparkman & Stephens designs for Nautor, in production at the famous Finnish yard from 1977 to 1984 with *Windsong* the 24th of the 29 models produced. She is owned by a prominent member of the New York Yacht Club, who keeps the yacht on the East Coast, at Pilot's Point Marina at Westbrook in Connecticut, as well as taking her to the Caribbean in the winter where she has raced at Antigua Sailing Week.

The 57s were both sloop and ketch rigged and were available in a centreboard version too. Two 57s took part in the Whitbread race during its Corinthian era: Norwegian Olympic medallist Peder Lunde racing *Berge Viking* to eighth place in the 1981/2 race and Swiss doctors Otto and Nora Zehender-Mueller achieving a 12th place finish with *Shadow of Switzerland* four years later.

LOA	57ft 4in	17.50m
LWL	45ft 8in	13.96m
Beam	15ft 8in	4.83m
Draught	9ft 1in	2.80m
Displacement	49,500lb	22,500kg
Sail area	1,462sqft	133.80m²
Designer	Sparkman & Stephens	
Builder	Nautor, Pietarsaari, Finland	
Launched	1979	

Group 4 page 105

For most, sailing around the world once, training up an amateur crew as you go, is sufficient. Mike Golding did that, taking second place to *Nuclear Electric* by just 2 hours 10 minutes in Chay Blyth's inaugural round the world race, the British Steel Challenge of 1992/3. *Group 4* was the only yacht to win two of the four legs and was denied almost certain overall victory by a rigging turnbuckle failure which required a diversion into the Brazilian port of Florianopolis. Golding did the race a second time, this time leading the 1996–7 BT Global Challenge from beginning to end. But as if that was not enough, Golding made a third circumnavigation in between, on his own, and with express intent of beating Chay Blyth's pioneering effort against the prevailing winds and currents back in 1968–9. Golding was only the second solo sailor to go round the world against the grain. His 167-day record was 125 days faster than Blyth's.

"The reasons have often been misinterpreted," explained Golding. "It's not just a question of improved technology or a larger yacht. These certainly had an effect, but the more important reason is simply to do with modern perceptions of what is possible. When Chay set out he was doing something that had never been done before. Like the first ascent of Everest the achievement was everything, the manner secondary."

Three decades before, solo sailors would often heave-to or run under bare poles in severe weather. Golding pressed on, the exceptionally tough yachts Blyth had created for his Challenge races uniquely suited to plugging away day-in, day-out. So too is Golding. A one time fire brigade watch leader, he is just the sort of resilient, resourceful stamped-from-a-solid-billet type of man to carry off such a voyage.

The *Group 4* yacht was modified quite modestly to turn her from a fully crewed yacht into one for a solo sailor: autopilot, roller furling jibs, spinnakers with squeezers, generator and a new bunk in the doghouse. Autopilot problems and a failed generator which had Golding on the brink of quitting through lack of electrical power were all overcome in what was a triumph for this very modest, very capable sailor.

LOA	67ft 0in	20.42m
LWL	55ft 0in	17.76m
Beam	17ft 3in	5.26m
Draught	9ft 6in	2.82m
Displacement	82,880lb	37,500kg
Sail area	1,932sqft	179.49m²
Designer	David Thomas	
Builder	DML, Plymouth	
Launched	1992	

Essex Girl page 106–7

Stephen Jones is probably Britain's most underrated designer, yet he is never one to shy away from drawing unusual yachts. *Essex Girl* is a case in point, commissioned by Richard Matthews, whose Oyster Marine produces a top line of large, cruising yachts, but whose name was made in the 1970s and '80s by successful racing hulls, the Jones-designed Oyster 41, 43 and SJ35 among them.

Speed was the paramount in *Essex Girl*'s creation, taking precedence over rating, though a weather eye was kept on the CHS (Channel Handicap System) and West Indies handicap. The hull is clean and lean, carrying a deep fin keel with a lead bulb and a powerful rig. *Essex Girl* can carry conventional spinnakers or be supercharged with asymmetric spinnakers flown off the end of a 17-foot bowsprit when some 3,688 square foot of sail can be carried. "She is one of the nicest, most vice-free sailing boats I have ever owned," says Richard Matthews, who has already clocked 22 knots in the boat. "She is beautifully balanced

and sails like a large dinghy flying across the water rather than ploughing her way through it," he adds. A rather different sensation from Richard Matthews' other racing yacht, the converted 12-metre *Crusader*, Britain's 1987 America's Cup challenger.

Unfortunately *Essex Girl* suffered major structural damage returning to England's east coast from Cowes Week in 1994 which lead to lengthy litigation between the yacht's owner and the material and specification provider. This has frustrated the hope that *Essex Girl* would compete on the Caribbean circuit. Despite the CHS rating system taking a dim view of *Essex Girl*'s design characteristics, piling on penalty after penalty, the yacht has sailed in the 1996 Rolex Commodores' Cup and won the Royal Ocean Racing Club's North Sea race overall and in a record elapsed time in the same season.

LOA	46ft 4in	14.11m
LWL	39ft 0in	11.88ft
Beam	13ft 1in	3.99m
Draught	9ft 7in	2.94m
Displacement	15,886lb	7,205kg
Sail area	1,182sqft	110m²
Designer	Stephen Jones	
Builder	Oyster Marine Special Projects/ Killian Bushe	
Launched	1994	

Silk 2 page 108–9

Here is the yacht made famous by Beken of Cowes, with a little help from *Silk*'s crew and the conditions on the Tuesday of Skandia Cowes Week 1996: a wind which had been blowing a steady 28 to 30 knots until a 40-knot squall raced down the Solent.

Silk 2 was running down the Solent near Stone Point on the mainland side, her crew stacked aft around helmsman Gordon Maguire. A 35-knot gust walloped the Bashford Howison 41 hard as she charged along under full main and 0.9 ounce asymmetric spinnaker. She recovered, and was in the process of shaking the water off like a dog, when a second, stronger gust hit and she nosedived. The only crew man forward, bowman Simon Corner found himself ten feet under. Maguire and the rest of the crew were suddenly 25ft in the air, wondering what was going to happen next. Remarkably the rig stayed intact and *Silk* slowly fell to leeward and ended up on her side, just as if she had broached normally. In the midst of all this Ed, son of *Silk 2*'s owner Jocelyn Waller, fell out of the cockpit where he had been tending the vang, on one side of the boat, which then slid over on top of him. Somehow he passed between the keel and rudder and popped up on the other side.

Ed Waller was in no danger and Ken Beken was standing by in his Boston Whaler boat, but Maguire and crew dropped the spinnaker and made several attempts to pick him up before deciding quite wisely to drop the sails, switch the engine on, retrieve Waller and motor back to Cowes. The only damage was to the pulpit and pushpit and one stanchion.

Despite the retirement, *Silk 2* won Cowes Week CHS Class 1, after an epic struggle with sistership *Wolf* (see page 97).

LOA	41ft 0in	12.50m
LWL	39ft 0in	11.88m
Beam	12ft 2in	3.70m
Draught	8ft 6in	2.60m
Displacement	15,400lb	7,000kg
Sail area	1,221sqft	113.50m²
Designer	Iain Murray & Associates	
Builder	Bashford Boat-Builders, Nowra, Australia	
Launched	1995	

Fazisi page 110

Remember when we knew little about the Soviet Union? There was Solzhenitsyn, Nureyev, news reports from Afghanistan, TV footage of the Politbureau atop Lenin's tomb for the May Day parade. If the West was ignorant, then imagine how the various republics knew next to nothing about us.

One of the early rumours of *Fazisi* was that she was drawn from designers learning about the IOR from a dog-eared copy of *Yachting World*. What was the incontrovertible truth was there was no yacht bigger than 54 feet in the USSR, yet here was an unbelievably ambitious plan to enter a maxi in the 1989–90 Whitbread.

This was the time of Gorbachev and *perestroika*, although the Communist party had still to be prised from power. Victor Tichov was the first Georgian entrepreneur to attempt a private enterprise joint venture and *Fazisi* was meant to show off Georgian aluminium boat-building technology. The hurdles to overcome were beyond comprehension so, no surprise then, that when *Fazisi* was flown by Antonov 124 transporter to Southampton six weeks before the start she was incomplete and rated a full three feet above the 70.05-foot IOR limit for a maxi. Swapping the keel for one discarded from the *Rothmans* maxi did the trick.

American Skip Novak had been brought in as firefighting consultant to get *Fazisi* ready for the race. He ended up co-skipper with Ukrainian Alexei Gryshenko. Against all odds, *Fazisi* made the start despite chronic money problems and then came fifth on the first leg to Uruguay. But the battle to make the boat ready, the months spent away from home and the suddenness of finding himself in the West proved too much for Gryshenko. He committed suicide. Remarkably the yacht finished the race, her crew made friends in every stop and *Fazisi*'s designer, Vladislav Murnikov, started a new life in the USA.

LOA	82ft 0in	25.00m
LWL	71ft 10in	21.90
Beam	19ft 0in	5.80m
Draught	12ft 4in	3.77m
Displacement	49,175lb	22,306kg
Sail area	2,790sqft	160m²
Designer	Vladislav Murnikov	
Builder	Poti Shipyard, Georgia	
Launched	1989	

Provezza Source page 112–13

During Denmark's keen interest in the Champagne Mumm Admiral's Cup in the late 1970s and early '80s, Victor Gruelich was a key player. He was his country's largest BMW dealer but had formed a successful relationship with Andels Bank to sponsor boats in 1987 and 1989. The partnership continued with a brand new custom Two Tonner for the 1991 season, though a series of acquisitions and mergers meant that Andels Bank was now Unibank and the yacht carried her backer's new logo, a unicorn's head, on her topsides.

Steered by Jens Christensen she was second to Guiseppe Degenarro's Italian yacht, *Larouge*, at the Two Ton Cup in Kiel two months before the 1991 Admiral's Cup but *Unibank* was brand new and seemed to be closing the gap on *Larouge* with every race. Come the Admiral's Cup, *Larouge* finished in front again, as did four other Two Tonners.

Soon after the series, *Unibank* was sold to Turkey, but returned for the 1993 Admiral's Cup to help out the host nation whose stock of grand-prix boats was down to one. Graham Walker, owner of the famous line of *Indulgence* yachts, saved the British from embarrassment by finding two yachts to join his 50-footer *Indulgence*, with Peter Morton arranging the charter of *Unibank*, now called *Provezza*, from Bulent Attaby, though it meant the British only got their hands on the boat a few days before the series itself. Stuart Childerley was skipper, joined by Kiwi America's Cup sailor Chris Dickson and between them they were not just the heaviest scorer in the British team but were fourth boat overall in the 23-boat fleet.

LOA	44ft 0in	13.43m
LWL	37ft 7in	11.50m
Beam	13ft 6in	4.13m
Draught	8ft 6in	2.62m
Displacement	19,400lb	8,800kg
Sail area	1,119sqft	104m²
Designer	Judel/Vrolijk	
Builder	Solution Composites, Cowes	
Launched	1991	

Omen pages 114–15

Omen enters the history books as the first example of the ILC40 class. This International Level Class was created in 1993 by the Offshore Racing Council to replace the old One Ton class when the IOR was replaced by the IMS as their worldwide rating rule for grand-prix racing. At the heart of IMS is a computer-run algorithm which can convert a numerical assessment of a yacht's design into a seconds-per-mile expression of its performance potential. In order to get different boats to race without handicap the ILC40s have to meet specified seconds-per-mile value over a range of wind speeds and sailing angles.

Omen was initially campaigned by German Thomas Friese in a complex charter/purchase deal with the yacht's builder, Carroll Marine of the USA, and he recruited the well-established pairing of helmsman Francesco de Angelis and tactician Torben Grael, normally found on the Italian Admiral's Cuppers *Mandrake* and *Brava*, to race her in the 1994 Rolex Commodores' Cup in Cowes. This they did with reasonable success, coming third for Germany's Red team out of nine contenders and placing seventh in the individual standings in the 27-boat fleet. *Omen* was sold to Irish owner Tony Mullins who renamed her *Rats on Fire* (perhaps because he had a weather eye on *Omen*'s sistership *Pigs in Space*) and in Ireland's line-up in the 1995 Champagne Mumm Admiral's Cup she was a creditable third in class.

LOA	40ft 9in	12.49m
LWL	36ft 3in	11.08m
Beam	13ft 1in	4.00m
Draught	7ft 8in	2.39m
Displacement	12,985lb	5,890kg
Sail area	11,937sqft	110.90m²
Designer	Bruce Farr & Associates	
Builder	Carroll Marine, Bristol, Rhode Island	
Launched	1994	

Fortuna page 116

Fortuna began life as the first Spanish designed and built maxi yacht and ended up four years later as a curious British failure. Javier Vissiers designed the boat to with an eye firmly on fresh to strong winds in the Whitbread of 1989–90 but unfortunately the percentages show that Whitbread boats don't spend that long in heavy going. When *Fortuna* did, she became "Flying" *Fortuna*, reeling off a 398-mile noon to noon run which, at the time, was a world record for a monohull. But there simply was not enough heavy running and reaching and *Fortuna*'s relatively light displacement meant that she had a modest amount of sail too and just could not hack it in light/medium conditions. Her maxi class results tell the story of her 1989–90 Whitbread performance well enough: 10 – 9 – 6 – 11 – 11 – 7 giving an eventual seventh overall.

Her skippers, Jan Santana and Javier de la Gandara, alternated with the latter having his hands full in Leg 2 in the Southern Ocean: a man overboard (successfully recovered) and three others with a broken leg, broken collar bone and dislocated shoulder.

For the 1993–4 Whitbread, she was taken over by British skipper Lawrie Smith. Try as he might he just could not raise sponsorship in Britain for his own maxi, which drew him towards Spain's biggest tobacco company, Tobacalera. Already, they had cut *Fortuna* in half, the work carried out by Vision Yachts, a new 12-foot fillet inserted in the hull and deck to lengthen her. Heavier now, the trade-offs in the IOR allowed Vissiers to add much needed sail area to the boat. Smith wanted more. He knew he wasn't going to win in a chopped-around old boat, so decided to play the joker and take a radical gamble. The underbody was reshaped from the keel forward, the stern extended and a huge composite wing-masted mizzen stepped, on which a cloud of sail could be crammed. This flying tooth-pick was designed by Ian Howlett and built by Carbospars of Hamble. With so much sail aloft, *Fortuna*'s decks seemed in a state of perpetual shadow.

The debut of *Fortuna* Mk III in the Fastnet Race was not auspicious: she was beaten not just by her maxi ketch rivals *Merit Cup*, *La Poste* and *New Zealand Endeavour* but the smaller Whitbread 60s having lacked bite upwind on the way to the Rock and blowing out her spinnakers and gennakers on the way back. The keel was changed in time for the Whitbread. *Fortuna* didn't fare any better. Little more than twenty-four hours into the race, the mizzen fell down off Ushant after the aluminium bumpkin at the stern, to which it was anchored and sheeted, failed. The maxi motored back to Hamble, when the main mast also dropped, probably from damage sustained in the mizzen failure. Tabacalera pulled the plug on the project.

LOA	81ft 2in	24.74m
LWL	64ft 6in	19.60m
Beam	19ft 0in	5.83m
Draught	12ft 8in	3.90m
Displacement	66,446lb	30,140kg
Sail area	3,670sqft	341m²

Designer	Javier Vissiers/Tony Castro/	
	Ian Howlett	
Builder	Mefasa, Spain/Vision Yachts, Cowes	
Launched	1988	

Ville de Paris page 117

Philippe Briand has been synonymous with France's America's Cup efforts since the mid 1980s, when Marc Pajot took the gun-metal grey *French Kiss* through to the Louis Vuitton Cup challenger semi-finals. Briand cut his America's Cup teeth with Swede Pelle Petterson and the *Sverige* 12-metre. But if there was a legacy left to modern French Cup efforts then it came from Baron Marcel Bich, the man who made a fortune from the ink the world's consumers left in Bic pens and our throw-away mentality which made disposable razors a hit.

Pajot's success has been remarkably varied: a 1972 Olympic silver medal with his brother Yves in the Flying Dutchman class, a watch captain in the first Whitbread race with Eric Tabarly and then domination of the big multihull ocean racing scene. His 65-foot catamaran *Elf-Aquitaine II* was a Briand design.

Ville de Paris was the third of three International America's Cup Class yachts built for Pajot's 1992 syndicate, which took its name from France's capital. Then mayor Jacques Chirac was a keen supporter. Briand's third design proved very competitive after a disappointing second boat, winning a place in the challenger semi-finals where she tied for last spot with Japan's *Nippon* with three wins to Italy's *Il Moro di Venezia*'s five wins and *New Zealand*'s seven.

But *Ville de Paris* was a well-regarded boat: with more time, more money, she could have fared better. In the autumn of 1992, she raced Elizabeth Meyer's 1934 Cup challenger, *Endeavour*, during La Nioulargue, to compare America's Cup design separated by more than 50 years. Although she is shown trailing *Endeavour* in this photograph, the newer yacht soon romped away.

LOA	77ft 6in	23.66m
LWL	62ft 4in	19.00m
Beam	18ft 0in	5.50m
Draught	13ft 1in	3.99m
Displacement	56,000lb	25,400kg
Sail area	3,509sqft	326m²
Designer	Philippe Briand	
Builder	MAG & VMG (hull) and Pinta (deck)	
Launched	1995	

Maiden pages 118–19

Throughout the 1980s and '90s, Bruce Farr was the dominant race boat designer. Few remember now his walkabout in the late '70s when he was fed up with constant changes by the rule makers which seem to penalize his boats in particular. They were different from the then norm: light displacement, fractionally-rigged, broad-sterned and shallow-floored. More dinghies than proper yachts, seemed the view of the rule-making establishment.

His designs *45° South*, *Gunboat Rangiriri*, *Joe Louis* and *The Red Lion* made a clean sweep of the Quarter, Half, Three-Quarter and One Ton Cups in the mid 1970s. "Marketwise, we were running into a problem. We found that when one of our boats was successful there would be a rule change," said a het-up Farr at the time. By 1978, he felt those administering the IOR were not playing with a straight bat. "Prior to then, the object of the rule was to encourage fair and equitable racing between boats of different styles. In effect, it encouraged development. But in 1978 the Rule Management Policy was introduced to correct the majority of the fleet. In effect they were trying to encourage the style of

boats of five years ago." Disenchanted, Farr designed many successful boat outside of the IOR in the 1978–80 period, until putting his toe back in the water with *Disque d'Or*, a specialized Whitbread boat for noted Swiss skipper Pierre Fehlmann. She was aimed at handicap honours, her 58-foot length and light-medium displacement targeted at easy surfing and hard driving due to the light loads of the fractional rig. Some of the light displacement concept was lost in her rugged aluminium, but she placed tenth in the 1981–2 Whitbread out of 27 boats, the race's biggest ever fleet.

In 1986, she raced around the world again, this time as *Stabilo Boss* in the hands of Bertie Reed, and laid up in Cape Town was where Tracy Edwards found her. Cook aboard *Atlantic Privateer* in the 1985–6 Whitbread, Edwards set about her pioneering all women's crew in the 1989–90 race. Immense persistence in the face of everything from scepticism to hostility saw *Maiden* make the start line, thanks to eleventh-hour sponsorship from Royal Jordanian Airlines, and achieve two wins and second overall in Class D; Edwards' own unswerving determination seeing the project through against all manner of odds.

Disque d'Or still bears the *Maiden* name, now owned by Terry Neilson of Edinburgh, who plies the pay-berth market. She was chartered by Stuart Bowen-Davis, owner of another former Whitbread yacht, *Creighton's Naturally*, for the 1996–7 Hong Kong Challenge amateur round the world race.

LOA	56ft 3in	17.71m
LWL	45ft 11in	13.75m
Beam	16ft 5in	5.03m
Draught	10ft 5in	3.20m
Displacement	48,000lb	21,773kg
Sail area	2,000sqft	185.80m²
Designer	Bruce Farr & Associates	
Builder	Chantier Pouvreau, La Rochelle, France	
Launched	1980	

New Zealand Endeavour   pages 120–21

Being the bridesmaid does not come easily to a one time power lifter, so Grant Dalton smarted when his *Fisher & Paykel* trailed Peter Blake's *Steinlager 2* around the world in the 1989–90 Whitbread race. "Coming second is not good enough – I, of all people, understand that," said Dalton as he laid plans for victory in the next Whitbread. "When you set a goal and don't quite reach it, you can't just set it aside, you can't be satisfied, you can't say 'The End'. And so it is for me and my team."

Peter Blake may have hung up his Whitbread sea boots by the time of the 1993–4 race, to concentrate on the Jules Verne Trophée and the America's Cup, but Dalton got his head down and mapped out a victory. He returned to designer Bruce Farr for one of three

brand new maxis built for the race. On her debut, *New Zealand Endeavour* took line honours in the Sydney–Hobart race in December 1992 and by early 1993 was lining up against her prospective Whitbread rivals in the Round Europe Race: Pierre Fehlmann's *Merit Cup* and Daniel Malle's *La Poste*. Dalton's select crew of New Zealanders trounced their European rivals and the calibre of his crew, particularly navigator Mike Quilter who, kept *New Zealand Endeavour* in the optimum winds, meant that Dalton went on to win the maxi class in the Whitbread race itself.

For Dalton, there was equal or greater competition from the smaller Whitbread 60 class because he always wanted to be first into each port and be fastest around the world: "That's what the public understand," asserted Dalton. Dalton's prime competition for this was the smaller Whitbread 60 class. Whilst developing *New Zealand Endeavour*'s design, Dalton spent US$60,000 racing the W60s in a computer simulation. Predicting the outcome, Dalton forecast: "In a breeze, they will beat us around the word. In the light we are quicker and I believe in the probability that a maxi will win overall." Strictly speaking there was no overall prize, only individual honours for the maxi class and the W60, but Dalton achieved his aim, *New Zealand Endeavour*'s combined time being 120 days 5 hours 9 minutes compared to W60 winner, *Yamaha*, completing the course in 120 days 14 hours 55 minutes. After the race, *New Zealand Endeavour* was sold to Norwegian Christian Medin.

LOA	84ft 4in	25.73m
LWL	65ft 3in	19.92m
Beam	18ft 6in	5.69m
Draught	12ft 0in	3.66m
Displacement	61,355lb	27,832kg
Sail area	4,036sqft	375.80m²
Designer	Bruce Farr & Associates	
Builder	Marten Marine, Auckland	
Launched	1992	

Sorcery   page 122

The early 1980s saw a burst of activity in the maxi class. For several seasons, the Ron Holland-designed boats *Kialoa IV* (owned by Jim Kilroy of Los Angeles) and *Condor* (owned by Briton Bob Bell) has ruled the roost and the big, red *Sorcery* was an attempt to prise apart their grip on the class.

She was designed by the late Gary Mull, a colourful Californian whose stories could be as tall as his moustache was wide. For many years he was chairman of the Offshore Racing Council's International Technical Committee, the inner cabal of those worthy administrators whose job it was to run the handicap rules for offshore racing around the world. Their annual meetings could be excruciatingly dull, as many a grey-headed, blue-blazered, well-meaning delegate argued over items of little relevance and ducked from clear decisions on important items. Mull's presentations and interventions were far more apposite and appetizing. His first and only maxi design did not hit the mark quite so well. She was commissioned by Jake Wood, whose business is in aircraft fastenings and he built her inside his Highland Park works in Los Angeles, trucking her through downtown LA for launching at Marina del Rey, where he owns a considerable number of docks. She made her debut at the 1994 Southern Ocean Racing Conference in Florida. *Sorcery* was a moderately conservative boat, unlike some of Mull's early boats, such as the lightweight flyer *La Forza del Destino*, but even so, Mull claimed his boat to have better sail area to displacement and sail area to

wetted surface ratios than the likes of *Kialoa IV* and *Condor*. Her mainsail hoist was the first to breech the 100-foot threshold at 101 feet, the equivalent of a five-story building, so you can imagine what it was like handling the jibs and spinnakers. One small comparison helps put the size of these boats into perspective: the twin foredeck hatches for sail handling were big enough to pass a VW Golf through. Wood still owns *Sorcery* and while her age gives her a generous rating, she remains no slouch. When she competed in the 1994 Round Ireland Race, she finished only 20 minutes behind the highly fancied *Longobarda*, yet beat her by something like eight hours on corrected time.

LOA	82ft 3in	25.08m
LWL	69ft 0in	21.03m
Beam	19ft 7in	6.00m
Draught	12ft 6in	3.81m
Displacement	79,621lb	36,126kg
Sail area	2,887sqft	268.20m²
Designer	Gary Mull	
Builder	Republic Yachts, Newbury, California	
Launched	1983	

Trader   page 123

Fred Detwiler, a Detroit businessman from the Trade Exchange of America, went to Estonia to have this Alan Andrews-designed 70-footer built from S-Glass, pvc foam and epoxy, with the boat shipped back from Tallinn, yachting venue of the 1980 Moscow Olympics, to the Great Lakes for commissioning.

Trader made her debut in the Lakes' big race, the Chicago–Mackinac, in 1993, winning her class on corrected time. This she followed up with another class win in the Point Huron–Mackinac race. Andrews is a West Coast designer who started off with a spell in Doug Peterson's office in San Diego and then branched out on his own in the MORC (Midget Offshore Racing Championship) in the early 1980s before progressing into IOR boats, cruiser-racers, the IMS and big, light displacement boats – "sleds" which are a feature of Californian racing.

Since her first season, *Trader* has raced in the Atlantic, Pacific, Caribbean and Great Lakes and Fred Detwiler has also cruised her in the Virgin Islands.

LOA	70ft 6in	21.48m
LWL	62ft 0in	18.89m
Beam	16ft 0in	4.87m
Draught	12ft 0in	3.65m
Displacement	34,200lb	15,513kg
Sail area	2,003sqft	186m²
Designer	Alan Andrews Yacht Design	
Builder	AKE, Tallinn, Estonia	
Launched	1993	

Sagamore   pages 124–5

Sagamore was one of the first glimmers that the maxi class, so long the pinnacle of the big boat racing scene until its decline and fall in early 1991, was undergoing regeneration. She also marked the return of the most famous design offices of the 20th century to top echelon racing: Sparkman & Stephens.

Sagamore was commissioned by Jim Dolan of Oyster Bay, New York, and launched in June 1995 from the Yachting Developments yard in Auckland run by Ian Cook and Jon Douglas. Big, black and beautiful, *Sagamore* was rapidly shipped to the UK, taking part in the Channel and Fastnet Races which sandwich Cowes Week. It was a spectacularly successful debut, with *Sagamore* winning the Channel Race and coming second overall in the Fastnet Race. She then headed to the South of France to become winner of her class at La Nioulargue in St Tropez, and a year later in 1996 scored further success in one of ocean racing's classic events as class winner of the 1996 Bermuda Race.

LOA	81ft 2in	24.74m
LWL	68ft 10in	21.00m
Beam	18ft 10in	5.76m
Draught	13ft 6in	4.13m
Displacement	63,000lb	28,576kg
Sail area	3,005sqft	279m²
Designer	Sparkman & Stephens	
Builder	Yachting Developments, Auckland	
Launched	1995	

Trekker 2 pages 126–7

In 1980s South Africa, it was every national serviceman's dream to be a sailing instructor or crew member on *Voortrekker* where she was used for coastal races such as the Agulhas Races and Double Cape Race from Cape Town to the Cape of Good Hope and back.

Voortrekker II was designed by Angelo Lavranos for the South African Defence Force's Sailing Association as a true multi-purpose boat, capable of short-handed and fully crewed racing as well as sail training. Built in the Navy dockyard at windy Simonstown in 1981, she was 60-foot LOA to fit the length limits for races such as the OSTAR and Round Britain.

Her first race was from Cape Town to Punta del Este in 1982, with Bertie Reed in charge. He was South Africa's best known big boat skipper, but the boat was rolled on the return leg, which proved her toughness. She was taken over by John Martin, a navy officer and protégé of Reed after the two men raced her in the 1982 two-handed Round Britain race. Martin took her to a second place finish in the 1984 OSTAR. Ahead of *Thursday's Child* for much of the race, Martin proved his grit by hand steering for the last part of the crossing due to autopilot failures.

In 1985, Martin teamed up with Boris Webber, later to skipper *Courtaulds International* in Chay Blyth's 1996–7 BT Global Challenge, before Lavranos updated the boat with a lighter keel and water ballast tanks. In this configuration, Martin and Rob Sharp broke the two-handed transatlantic record in 1986. Later that year, Martin set off alone from Newport, Rhode Island, in the BOC solo round the world race. Renamed *Tuna Marine*, he won legs 1 and 4 yet had to be content with fifth overall thanks to two grim Southern Ocean legs when mainsail damage and broken running backstay slowed him. Undaunted, Martin posted another second in the 1988 OSTAR. The 4000-litre inside ballast

tanks were removed, a heavier keel fitted and a new interior built in 1991 by her second owner Alf Duncan. The stern scoop was made permanent as was the name change to *Trekker 2*.

LOA	64ft 3in	19.60m
LWL	53ft 8in	16.40m
Beam	14ft 7in	4.50m
Draught	11ft 8in	3.60m
Displacement	36,155lb	16,400kg
Sail area	1,937sqft	180m²
Designer	Angelo Lavranos	
Builder	SA Navy, Simonstown	
Launched	1981	

NCB Ireland page 128

To finish 12th out of 15 maxis in the 1989–90 Whitbread can't be called a success in competitive terms, but what *NCB Ireland* achieved was remarkable enough. Thanks to backing from the likes of Howard Kilroy of Jefferson Smurfitt, Dermot Desmond of National City Brokers and a whole phalanx of supporters, Ireland managed to build its own maxi boat and race it with a 50 per cent Irish crew under Cork's Joe English in the biggest round the world race of all. In itself, that was no mean achievement.

The *NCB Ireland* project was launched on a wet, windy Dublin day by Charles Haughey, keen sailor and then the Irish premier. Interest at home was keen, thanks in part to the imaginative idea of trailering the building plug for the boat, painted up like a real hull, around Ireland as part of a roadshow. The Electrical Supply Board, a co-sponsor, helped out by cutting and re-connecting overhead power lines when the going got tricky. One side of the plug was detachable to negotiate some of the Ireland's narrower roads.

Ron Holland tipped the design towards the greater proportion of reaching and running in the Whitbread race, whilst retaining the displacement and stability for an upwind edge. She was a conventional sloop-rigged maxi like *Rothmans*, *Martela OF* and *Merit Cup*, whom she struggled to match for pace, but ultimately all three were simply outclassed by the Kiwi ketches *Steinlager 2* and *Fisher & Paykel*.

LOA	80ft 10in	24.25m
LWL	66ft 5in	20.26m
Beam	20ft 0in	6.09m
Draught	13ft 0in	3.96m
Displacement	69,440lb	31,564kg
Sail area	4,015sqft	373m²
Designer	Ron Holland	
Builder	Killian Bushe & Rob Lipsett	
Launched	1989	

Steinlager 2 page 129

If you want to raise the bar room temperature in Auckland amongst Whitbread salts, a good question to drop into conversation is: "Who thought of the ketch rig first – Peter Blake or Grant Dalton?" The discussion hinges around the two Kiwi ketches which dominated the 1989–90 Whitbread round the world race, Blake's *Steinlager 2* and Dalton's *Fisher & Paykel*, with *Steinlager* winning every leg and outright victory, a feat never achieved before in five races since 1973–4.

The Farr office is famous for its Chinese walls to protect the confidentiality of one client's design against that of another. By the same token, the Kiwi sailor's grapevine is one of the most efficient communication systems in the world so each would have had shrewd idea that the other was looking at a ketch rig

and that most of their European rivals were building sloops. It was a masterstroke because in the predominantly off-wind Whitbread course, the ketch could pile on more sail than the sloops and, better still, get much of it very "cheaply" under the IOR rating system. When the boats were "venetian blind-sailing" with five sails set, nothing could touch them.

Blake and his navigator Mike Quilter knew they had something special when they left the Farr office in Annapolis, Maryland. Blake, it seemed, had a gut feeling about making his ketch a fractional rig, whereas the Farr preferred option seemed to be a masthead rig configuration like Dalton's. "My father has had a fractional ketch for the past 30 years," Blake said at the time, "and when she competes against her sistership, a masthead ketch, she always beats her with a big margin."

In Farr's computer simulations, the margins that *Steinlager 2* could achieve were staggering. Some rating benefit was gained by exploiting an IOR MkIIIa loophole, which saw *Steinlager 2* built three feet longer than *Fisher & Paykel*, 7,000 pounds heavier, yet carry proportionately much, much more sail: some 312 square feet upwind and 600 square feet downwind.

Reality proved as good as the projections. "Big Red" scored a crushing victory, though not without a scare one week from the finish when a mizzen chainplate failed. Reflex action by Brad Butterworth on the helm saved the rig, and race, from disaster. Perhaps she was a lucky boat. The first hull delaminated during construction following a resin failure. But not even this could stop Blake's crew. A second hull was built in double-quick time, a pace the boat maintained as soon as she hit the water. After the race, *Steinlager 2* was sold to Italy's Giorgio Falck, who raced her as *Safilo*, before selling her to Vassart Marine Charter of Belgium.

LOA	83ft 6in	25.49m
LWL	66ft 5in	20.29m
Beam	18ft 9in	5.76m
Draught	13ft 0in	3.99m
Displacement	77,551lb	35,177kg
Sail area	4,412sqft	409.90m²
Designer	Bruce Farr & Associates	
Builder	Southern Pacific Boatyard, Auckland	
Launched	1988	

Longobarda pages 130–31

If you want to make a statement *Longobarda* is a pretty good way of doing it. Built for Gianni Varasi, an Italian with a glass business in Europe, the USA and South America plus other interests in chemicals, publishing and property, the bright white maxi was launched on 17 July 1989 and won her first race on 2 August. She eventually won all three rounds of that season's Maxi World Championships in Mallorca, Porto Cervo and St Tropez. The size of the margin for overall victory was a crushing 29.25 points over Raul Gardini's *Il Moro di Venezia*, and this is a class where boats were regarded as needing a full season to work up to their potential.

Designed by Bruce Farr, she was his first fractionally-rigged maxi, was built light but relatively heavy in displacement, and lacked for nothing in terms of high calibre crew. American John Bertrand guided *Longobarda* to her early successes. *Matador²* was top maxi in 1991 but the class withered away as key owners such as Raul Gardini and Bill Koch concentrated on their 1992 America's Cup campaigns. Briton Mike Slade found *Longobarda* looking forlorn, laid up ashore in Antibes in late 1993, but with two containers full of sails and gear. A key objective was the New York YC's 150th anniversary regatta in Newport, Rhode Island where, lined up against *Matador²* again, the honours were shared.

Longobarda was then trucked to the San Francisco Big Boat series before heading to Australia for the fiftieth Sydney–Hobart race.

"Technically, it's been quite an exciting project," says Mike Slade of the changes he and consultant Hugh Welbourn have wrought. Their aim has been to turn a boat not only designed to the IOR rating rule but the specialist requirements of windward/leeward racing on inshore courses in light to medium conditions, into a boat competitive under the IMS rating. Purpose-built IMS maxis are beamier and lighter than *Longobarda* but even so, her displacement has been reduced by 8 tons to 30 tons while her sailing length has grown by 4 feet 6 inches. Returning from the 1995 Sydney–Hobart, *Longobarda* narrowly escaped a pirate attack off Somalia. Once back in the UK she underwent extensive hull modifications, beating the Round the Island Race record in 1996 (held by Mike Slade's 80-foot *Ocean Leopard*), while over the winter 1996-7, Hugh Welbourn designed another round of hull modifications.

LOA	79ft 8in	24.32m
LWL	65ft 6in	20.00m
Beam	19ft 10in	6.09m
Draught	14ft 2in	4.31m
Displacement	84,215lb	38,200kg
Sail area	4,206sqft	390.83m²
Designer	Bruce Farr & Associates	
Builder	SAI Ambrosini, Italy	
Launched	1989	

Aerosail   page 132

When Daimler-Benz announced long-term sponsorship of German sailing, from the Olympic classes, through the Mumm 36 and offshore classes such as the ILC40 (International Level Class) and with a long-range goal of an America's Cup challenge, it seemed the sport worldwide was moving up a gear. Sponsorship from a high technology company which wanted to apply its resources was rather different from the billboard norm of sailing sponsorship and, outside of the America's Cup, was exceptional.

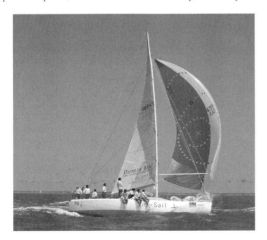

Triple gold medallist Jochen Schumann was put in charge of the sailing team and briefed to focus on bringing the younger generation of sailors through. Managing the business side of the *Aerosail* project was vastly more complex. Bosses came and went and the atmosphere got distinctly more political as money was spent but results were hard to come by. Increasingly the imperative of training crew and achieving short term results were mutually exclusive until the Daimler-Benz board, facing losses, plant closures and hot potatoes such as the failure of their Dutch subsidiary Fokker, aborted the project in November 1995, three years after it had started. *Aerosail Astro* was the first of two ILC40s built and designed by Judel/Vrolijk with input from Heiner Meldner. She raced for Germany in the 1994 Rolex Commodores' Cup, where the German Green team were runners up with *Astro* third in the middle class, and under charter to the British team in the 1995 Champagne Mumm Admiral's Cup, where she came last amongst seven newer rivals.

LOA	41ft 0in	12.50m
LWL	36ft 1in	11.00m
Beam	13ft 1in	4.00m
Draught	7ft 8in	2.40m
Displacement	12,566lb	5,600kg
Sail area	1,033sqft	96m²
Designer	Judel/Vrolijk	
Builder	Marten Marine, Auckland	
Launched	1994	

Aquitaine Innovations   page 133

Characteristic of a yacht so extreme, *Aquitaine Innovations* was dismasted in her first race, the 1996 Europe-1 STAR singlehanded transatlantic race, before vindicating those who put faith in her radical concepts by winning the Open 60 class in the 1997 Fastnet Race and, two months later, brushing the same rivals aside in the two-handed Transat Jacques Vabre from Le Havre to Cartegena in Colombia. In that race, and during the Fastnet, she was sailed by skipper Yves Parlier, nicknamed "ET, the Extra Terrestrial" by his fellow French sailors for his prowess at analysing and predicting the weather, and Eric Tabarly, whose rise to prominence in the very first solo transatlantic race in 1960 proved such a powerful influence on the generations of French sailors who followed.

Twinning Parlier and Tabarly in the Jacques Vabre was a sponsor's dream and sure-fire crowd pleaser. The throng around *Aquitaine Innovations* in Le Havre proved the point. Setting this yacht apart is her rig which applies multihull thinking to a monohull. A normal monohull rig is limited in terms of its support by the width of the hull. Multihulls have a huge beam to provide as wide a staying base, so their spars can be much more radical, often wing shape in section and lighter in construction because the compression loads on them are less. This is what Parlier fitted to *Aquitaine Innovations*, a huge rotating wing mast whose cloud of sail would do justice to a 90-footer never mind a 60-footer. To generate as wide a staying base as possible for the mast, the shrouds are lead to 15 foot long struts, appearing moustache-like from either side of the mast's base. From the stern, she looks like a beam trawler.

All this was put on top of a hull from Jean-Marie Finot and Pascale Conq, who seemed to have become the designers of choice for Open 60 yachts, thanks to a trio of victories in the big solo round the world races: Christophe Auguin's *Groupe Sceta* and *Sceta Calberson* in the 1990–91 and 1994–5 BOC Race and Alain Gautier's *Baggages Superior* in the 1992–3 Vendée Globe. They have learned how to make massively wide hulls track straight and true whilst heeled, essential for sailing with autopilots. Where their first hulls weighed 12 tons and could carry 6 tons of inside water ballast, Parlier managed to build *Aquitaine Innovations* at just 7 tons and use a swinging keel to do away with water ballast.

LOA	60ft 0in	18.28m
LWL	60ft 0in	18.28m
Beam	19ft 3in	5.90m
Draught	13ft 4in	4.10m
Disp	15,680lb	7,000kg
Sail area	3,745 sqft	348 m²
Designer	Group Finot	
Builder	JMV, Cherbourg	
Launched	1996	

Corum Saphir   pages 134–5

Capricorno grabbed the headlines, almost from the moment she was launched, when she was involved in a big collision during the 1991 50-foot regatta in Miami which knocked her bow clean off. So it was back to Eric Goetz's boatyard in Bristol, Rhode Island, at which she had been completed just three months before.

The glories came later. Built for Italy's Renaldo del Bono, she carried the yellow colours of the Corum Sailing Team as *Corum Saphir* and raced for France in both the 1991 and 1993 Champagne Mumm Admiral's Cup, spearheading an effort which made the French surprise winners in 1991. It started in the long inshore race in Hayling Bay when, as the sea breeze came in from seaward, *Corum Saphir* tacked right in underneath the cliffs on the Isle of Wight and, to the dismay of her rivals, came out smelling of roses. Backed up by team mates, the French team moved up to fourth and overcame a 20-point deficit to overhaul the Italians in the Fastnet race. This Philippe Briand-designed 50-footer was always excellent offshore, being a formidable reaching boat, but in the 1991 Admiral's Cup she displayed all round form: top inshore 50-footer (4 – 2 – 2 – 1) and top offshore 50-footer (3 – 1).

Her long competitive life continued after the Admiral's Cup when she raced in the 1994 Rolex Commodores' Cup, after changes from the IOR to the IMS, in Germany as *Antibody*.

LOA	50ft 7in	15.46m
LWL	42ft 7in	13.05m
Beam	15ft 1in	4.60m
Draught	9ft 4in	2.85m
Displacement	26,399lb	11,975kg
Sail area	1,829sqft	170m²
Designer	Philippe Briand	
Builder	Eric Goetz, Bristol, Rhode Island	
Launched	1990	

Maximiser   pages 136–7

The *Yeoman* name is synonymous with Britain's Aisher family and *Maximiser* started life as the latest in the one of the longest lines of yachts in the world: *Yeoman XXX*. After years of offshore racing in the English Channel and Admiral's Cup competition, Robin Aisher commissioned 73-foot *Yeoman XXX* from Bruce Farr as a fast cruiser for warm-water racing. The Caribbean circuit held special allure. She was built by South African Eric Bongers, himself a member of another famous sailing family, and launched in 1990. Her early life was plagued by misfortune. After competing in Antigua Week, *Yeoman XXX* was dismasted between Antigua and Bermuda when the mast heel support failed. The spar broke above the deck and had to be cut away. Adding ignominy to injury, *Yeoman XXX* was then rammed by a US Coast Guard cutter and was shipped back to the UK for repairs by Hamble Yacht Services.

Robin Aisher had her back in commission for the 1993 Fastnet Race but sold her the next year to another Briton, John Caulcutt, who renamed her *Maximiser*. He had her rattling around Ireland as *Virgin City Jet* in 1994 in the Cork Dry Gin race and then crossed the Atlantic in the Mount Gay Barbados Challenge in January 1995. She raced in Antigua both that year and in 1996, when she memorably won her class, the rest of the fleet having started at the wrong time and been disqualified. Being a blowy race, *Maximiser* sailed the course without a mainsail to collect maximum points with minimum effort. In 1996, Argentine Alberto Roemmers bought her and has continued to race her in the Caribbean, winning her class in the 1997 St Maarten regatta.

LOA	73ft 5in	22.40m
LWL	67ft 0in	18.60m
Beam	16ft 6in	5.05m
Draught	12ft 6in	3.85m
Displacement	60,032lb	27,300kg
Sail area	2,600sqft	241m²
Designer	Bruce Farr & Associates	
Builder	Eric Bongers, Cape Town	
Launched	1990	

The Card page 138

This Swedish maxi was a bit player in the sloop versus ketch contest which was a hallmark of the 1989–90 Whitbread round the world race for, although she was a ketch like the all-conquering boats from New Zealand – Peter Blake's *Steinlager 2* and Grant Dalton's *Fisher & Paykel* – she had much more sloop feel. She was shorter, lighter and carried less sail than either of the Kiwi ketches, less indeed than Pierre Fehlmann's sloop *Merit Cup*.

American John Baker had got the ball rolling with this boat, a businessman who was one of the very first pioneering the concept of leveraged buyouts in corporate raiding. Retired and a yachtsman, he looked upon the Whitbread as a project to sink his teeth into. Fellow American and three-time Whitbread competitor, Skip Novak, was his right-hand man. The boat started to build at Eric Goetz's yard in Bristol, Rhode Island not long after Wall Street's Black Friday of 19 October 1987. That, coupled with corporate America's lack of interest in stumping up $4 million plus of sponsorship for a British race, taking place on the world's oceans, and receiving minimal media coverage in the USA, meant the project was up for sale.

The yacht became *The Card* when Novak's navigator from the previous Whitbread, Swedish doctor Roger Nilson, won backing from Mastercard and raced the boat under Swedish colours finishing fifth behind *Steinlager 2* and *Fisher & Paykel*, plus the sloops *Merit Cup* and *Rothmans*. The sloop versus ketch debate took an unexpected twist during the fourth leg start from Auckland, when *The Card* swept past a 28-foot cruising boat which had come into the start box. The effect of the big boat sweeping past was first to roll the cruiser away and then back into the big yellow maxi. *The Card*'s mizzen mast rigging hooked the cruising boat, hauled her onto her beam ends whilst pulling the after mast out of the maxi. She completed the leg as a sloop. The mizzen was recovered and shipped to the next stop in Punta del Este.

Teddy Turner, son of the CNN/Warner Bros magnate Ted Turner, bought the boat after the race but the plan to race her as *Challenge America* in the 1993–4 Whitbread fell through.

LOA	78ft 8in	24.03m
LWL	63ft 4in	19.32m
Beam	18ft 5in	5.63m
Draught	13ft 5in	4.13m

Displacement	66,146lb	30,012kg
Sail area	4,021sqft	373.60m²
Designer	Bruce Farr & Associates	
Builder	Eric Goetz Boatworks, Bristol, Rhode Island	
Launched	1990	

Great News II page 139

This yacht grew out of a middle-of-the-road British cruiser-racer, the Sigma 38. Computer software giant Oracle told the RAF that if their Sigma 38 *Red Arrow* performed well enough, they would go on to greater things. In the hands of civvy helmsman Tim Law and RAF Sailing Association skipper Flight Lieutenant John Best, *Red Arrow* had an immensely successful season on the Sigma 38 circuit. As a result a brand-new Bruce Farr-designed 45-foot grand-prix race was commissioned and as the only Two-Tonner being built in Britain, she was assured of her place in the host nation's Admiral's Cup team for 1991. But the promise of the Sigma 38 campaign was never fulfilled in the vastly more complex Two-Tonner when it was raced in the more rarified level of elite competition. Observers suggested as much before the yacht ever went racing and *Wings of Oracle*'s failure to reach her potential became a self-fulfilling prophecy, despite spending the winter in Mallorca training.

A huge £1.2 million budget demanded results and they did not come. Nor was there any one to grapple with the complexities of the rating and sail development programmes. After a disappointing Two Ton Cup, Tim Law left the programme and olympic Finn-class dinghy sailor Stuart Childerley was brought in. By then it was probably too late to turn things around and *Wings of Oracle* finished sixth out of eighth in her class in Admiral's Cup. She was snapped up after the series by Australian John Calvert-Jones, Rupert Murdoch's brother-in-law, and renamed *Great News II*, but that was not enough to improve her fortune. She had only a moderate Admiral's Cup two years later, the low point of which was a dismasting in the Fastnet Race. She is now owned by another Australian, Geoff Wilson.

LOA	43ft 9in	13.39m
LWL	36ft 1in	11.02m
Beam	13ft 8in	4.22m
Draught	8ft 7in	2.67m
Displacement	17,795lb	8,072kg
Sail area	1,369sqft	127.20m²
Designer	Bruce Farr & Associates	
Builder	Green Marine, Lymington	
Launched	1991	

Ragamuffin pages 140–41

Built as *Will* for her Japanese owner, she was the definitive carbon fibre yacht. Everywhere the eye falls, there is an item made from the black, magic material: the steering wheel, winch grinding pedestal, guy blocks, stern light bracket, bunk frames, companionway ladder and, of course, the kitchen sink.

It seems bizarre that a racing yacht should be known for the black bucket in her minimalist galley but that's the truth. Built over the winter of 1990–91, this Bruce Farr-designed 50-footer was created for Ryouji Oda, textile manufacturer and supplier of futons to the Japanese Imperial household, for US$700,000. It was a fixed price contract, so with her Sydney builder geared to build the boat from carbon fibre, it made just as much sense to use

the material for ancillary items. Not that the sink was used: rules required it, but the only food ever consumed was pre-prepared.

More seriously, *Will* was built from very high modulus carbon fibre, pre-impregnated cloth kept at a low temperature to retard the start of the curing process, until it was vacuumed down over the mould. Then it was baked to cure the resin, tidied up and finally post-cured with a second baking. Her construction, an immensely strong structure, marked the zenith of IOR design. From the late '80s until 1992, the 50-foot class was hottest in terms of design and calibre of sailors. The rule died soon afterwards, ironically, just when racing between disparate designs was at its closest.

Will was sold to veteran Australian Syd Fischer, a Sydney property developer whose string of *Ragamuffins* had competed in the classic Fastnet and Sydney–Hobart races since the 1960s. A more enthusiastic advocate for offshore racing would be hard to find, so it was a fitting reward that *Will*, renamed *Ragamuffin*, won the Hobart race in 1993 at Fischer's 21st attempt. Fischer rebuilt the boat in 1995, changing her hull to suit the IMS which replaced the IOR as the grand-prix race rule, with the boat becoming fractionally longer and lighter with less upwind sail area but appreciably more downwind sail area.

LOA	49ft 7in	15.15m
LWL	40ft 4in	12.32m
Beam	14ft 9in	4.56m
Draught	9ft 6in	2.95m
Displacement	25,945lb	11,769kg
Sail area	1,771sqft	164.56m²
Designer	Bruce Farr & Associates	
Builder	McConaghy Boats, Sydney	
Launched	1991	

Charles Jourdan page 142

The individual leg results of the 1989–90 Whitbread tell the *Charles Jourdan* story pretty well. On Legs 2 and 4, the long stages through the Southern Ocean, French skipper Alain Gabbay brought *Charles Jourdan* home in fifth place both times. On the other legs, where there was more upwind sailing and a wider range of wind strengths, the yacht struggled with eleventh, ninth, twelfth and thirteenth place finishes. The reason? *Charles Jourdan* really was too small, too light and too much of a one-condition boat to perform consistently enough day-in and day-out in a 130-day race. It was a brave approach by Gabbay and ever-inventive designer Guy Ribadeau-Dumas. Because of the way the IOR treated light boats, *Charles Jourdan* was 10 feet shorter than her maxi class rivals and with only a modest sail plan: the reason why

she flew when it blew, but laboured elsewhere. "We take another philosophy from the maxis," explained Gabbay. "She is approximately half the weight of the other maxis. We have made the boat to race downwind, very fast, although we have some problems to make the same speed as the other maxis upwind and reaching."

An abiding memory of the 1989–90 Whitbread was when *Charles Jourdan* hit a whale in the Tasman Sea on the short Fremantle-Auckland stage. Hamming it up for the on board video cameraman, Gabbay, with his habitual cigarette in mouth, showed the gaping hole in the hull side, before peeling back the flapping laminate and flicking his ash out into the ocean beyond.

Charles Jourdan was revamped for the 1995 season for the Pharmacia-Upjohn company by Finnish designer Lussi Mannenberg, making a big impact during Cowes Week and winning the Fastnet Race when, in a lightening breeze she pulled clear of the other boats in Christchurch Bay and thereafter sailed in a different breeze.

LOA	72ft 2in	22.00m
LWL	66ft 11in	20.40m
Beam	17ft 4in	5.30m
Draught	9ft 10in	3.02m
Displacement	40,344lb	18,300kg
Sail area	2,692sqft	150m²
Designer	Guy Ribadeau-Dumas	
Builder	Nordahl Mabire	
Launched	1989	

Fisher & Paykel   page 143

Sponsored by New Zealand's biggest white goods firm, *Fisher & Paykel* became known the world-over by her Kiwi vowel-slaughtering name of *"Fisher & Pie-kel"* and for her epic duel in the 1989–90 Whitbread race with Peter Blake's *Steinlager 2*.

Fisher & Paykel was Grant Dalton's first Whitbread as skipper, having cut his teeth as a sailmaker eight years previously on board the line honours and handicap-winning Dutch maxi *Flyer 2* and as a watch leader for Peter Blake four years later on *Lion New Zealand*. Stepping out of the shadow of one so tall and illustrious was always going to put the spotlight on Dalton and he responded with a thoroughly professional, hard-driven campaign.

Ultimately, *Fisher & Paykel* was beaten by *Steinlager 2* on Bruce Farr's design-office drawing table, as were the other new maxis in the race: *Rothmans, Merit Cup, The Card, Defender, Charles Jourdan, Fortuna Extra Lights, NCB Ireland* and *Martela OF,* though *Fisher & Paykel* was the one yacht which posed a continual threat to Blake's *Steinlager 2*. The reason was rig choice. Dalton's campaign developed two designs for the predicted conditions on the Whitbread course, which raced in Farr's computer to give a time around the world of 140 days. Dalton decided to try something radical and put a ketch rig on the hull in place of the fractional sloop. The new time was 135 days. Unsure whether to believe the numbers he plumped for the masthead rig ketch two days before building started. That put *Fisher & Paykel* ahead of all the field save *Steinlager 2*, where a similar thought process lead Blake to a fractional ketch on a longer, heavier hull.

Breaking the mizzen six days out from the first leg stopover over Punta del Este, Uruguay, hindered *Fisher & Paykel* placing her fourth on Leg 2 after which a pattern emerged: Dalton's yacht would work out a lead and hold it for much of the leg but as the winds lightened nearer land, *Steinlager 2* would pull through to make a clean sweep of all six legs. Dalton's yacht finished second overall, 36 hours behind *Steinlager 2*, and was sold to Spain's Jan Santana.

LOA	81ft 11in	24.98m
LWL	65ft 4in	19.90m
Beam	18ft 6in	5.66m
Draught	15ft 7in	3.85m
Displacement	70,357lb	31,914kg
Sail area	3,984sqft	370m²
Designer	Bruce Farr & Associates	
Builder	Marten Marine, Auckland	
Launched	1988	

Bellavista   page 144

Vittorio Moretti already owned a large Bruce Farr-designed racing yacht, built at his own Maxi Dolphin yard and named *Carmen di Bellavista* after his eldest daughter when he chartered another yacht for the 1992 season.

She was probably Italy's most famous grand-prix maxi yacht, launched as *Il Moro di Venezia III* in 1987 for flamboyant industrialist Raul Gardini, then head of the giant Montedison agrochemical business. In hiring Californian Paul Cayard as his skipper, he laid the foundations for Italy's first America's Cup challenge, an $80 million effort which constructed a boatyard in Venice to build five hulls and which came from behind against New Zealand in the challenger finals to win the right to challenge Bill Koch's *America³* in the Cup match, ultimately losing 1:4.

The German Frers-designed maxi was the springboard for that campaign, winning 1988 Maxi Worlds and San Francisco Big Boat Series. In the Spring of 1990 *Il Moro di Venezia III* was sold to Massimo Gatti as his new *Vanitas* and it was from him that Vittorio Moretti chartered the boat, renaming her *Vanita di Bellavista* to reflect the two strands of her ownership.

LOA	79ft 6in	24.28m
LWL	65ft 6in	20.00m
Beam	20ft 5in	6.24m
Draught	13ft 6in	4.15m
Displacement	78,483lb	35,600kg
Sail area	3,001sqft	278.70m²
Designer	German Frers	
Builder	SAI Ambrosini, Italy	
Launched	1987	

Container   page 145

The name was not especially elegant but the string of yachts owned by German Udo Schutz were remarkably effective. His business was industrial containers and storage vessels for substances

such as chemicals, hence the name of his yachts. Romance aside, his various *Containers* were always campaigned hard, increasing in size from 43-footers in the early 1980s to a pair of 50-footers, both designed by Judel/Vrolijk and built as his own Schutzwerke in Selters. Danish sailmaker Jens Christensen was the man charged with getting the results, being *Container*'s regular helmsman. *Container* never quite managed to break the hegemony of the Reichel/Pugh-designed pair of *Abracadabra* and *Champosa* when the IOR 50-foot class was at is zenith in the early 1990s, but she was the cornerstone of Germany's victorious 1993 Champagne Mumm Admiral's Cup team, being the second highest scorer in the series.

LOA	49ft 7in	15.11m
LWL	41ft 2in	12.55m
Beam	13ft 1in	4.00m
Draught	7ft 8in	2.40m
Displacement	24,911lb	11,300kg
Sail area	1,453sqft	135m²
Designer	Judel/Vrolijk	
Builder	Schutzwerke, Selters, Germany	
Launched	1991	

Congere   page 146–7

Congere slotted into a line of distinguished maxi yachts from German Frers, a masthead-rigged yacht like *Boomerang, Matador, Ondine IV* and *Kialoa V* and ahead of the later fractionally-rigged yachts such as *Il Moro di Venezia* and *Emeraude*, yet she was never campaigned with quite the same elan as her peers. Launched in later 1987, her life was brief but incident-filled: she was wrecked three seasons later. On 5 February, this German Frers-designed 77-footer ran aground on a sandbank, some 250 miles south of Rio Grande, Brazil, while competing in the Buenos Aires–Rio de Janeiro race.

The sudden deceleration and whiplash up the mast, broke the spar above the checkstays, though the crew were able to tidy up the debris and, importantly, prevent the mast from punching a whole in the hull's thin aluminium plating. One of *Congere*'s crew was able to swim to land – not much more than an Olympic medallist's javelin throw away – with a line, thus enabling all 25 crew members to be disembarked safely and without anyone being hurt. *Congere* was not so lucky, bouncing in the shore break, and losing her keel after some six to seven hours. The 77-foot maxi fetched up on the beach herself, a sand filled total loss. Her American owner, Bevan Koeppel, founder of the 7-Eleven convenience-store chain, replaced her with *Drumbeat*, a David Pedrick-designed maxi built for Australian America's Cup winner Alan Bond, after his business empire collapsed.

LOA	77ft 0in	23.49m
LWL	63ft 0in	19.20m
Beam	19ft 3in	5.88m
Draught	13ft 1in	3.95m
Displacement	88,183lb	19,640kg
Sail area	2,874sqft	267m²
Designer	German Frers	
Builder	Merrifield Roberts, Newport, Rhode Island	
Launched	1987	

America³   page 148

The America's Cup has been a magnet for all types of larger than life personalities: Lord Dunraven, Sir Thomas Sopwith, Frank Packer, Ted Turner, Alan Bond, to name only a handful.

In 1992 there was Bill Koch, who pulled off one of the most improbable victories. He had a huge ego and strong will that bent to no one, but a smaller than life personality, an "aw shucks" style of gentleness and extreme courtesy: a fascinating combination. Too many dismissed Koch as a lightweight. He was fabulously wealthy thanks to his father's coke-cracking business but had sued two of his brothers for an increased share of the inheritance, an action which popped him from the obscurity of Kansas roots and straight into the feature pages of *Vanity Fair*. Koch often made naïve statements – "I threw a party to see how many people we had on the *America¹* payroll – 300 turned up" – which fuelled an almost universal underestimation of what his America's Cup team was capable of.

But amid the rush to build three new hulls Koch assembled a hugely impressive design and technology group under the leadership of Jerry Milgram from Massachusetts Insitute of Technology and Heiner Meldner, who had worked on many black projects for the US Department of Defence. Among the yacht designers involved were John Reichel, Jim Pugh, Doug Peterson, Penn Edmunds and Jim Taylor. The result of all this science was *America¹*, a yacht faster than all the others in San Diego in 1992 and whose designers had such a clear and accurate grasp on their theoretical modelling, that they could design changes in the computer and know, for sure, they would work out at full size. It's hard to imagine, but the last change to *America¹* was made just two days before the America's Cup. The keel lead bulb was still warm from its casting when it was delivered to the Cuben compound.

The measure of Koch's achievement was not that he beat the Italian challenger, *Il Moro di Venezia V* 4:1 in a demonstrably one-sided series, but that he'd created a yacht fast enough for him, a modestly able Corinthian helmsman, to be able to steer in yachting's biggest competition and beat one of the world's best professionals, Californian Paul Cayard, who had been hired by the Italians. Koch's no rock-star sailors and Teamwork-Talent-Technology *modus operandi* worked like a dream in 1992. It had done so earlier, when Koch conquered another field which his maxi *Matador²* whose back-to-back world championships in 1990 and 1991 rendered the rest of the class obsolete. Much of that technology transferred into the 1992 Cup programme. Yet three years later, the Technology part of it could not create a boat fast enough for his Women's Team – the first in the America's Cup – to win the defender selection series which selects the yacht to defend the America's Cup.

LOA	75ft 5in	23.00m
LWL	53ft 1in	18.00m
Beam	15ft 10in	4.60m
Draught	13ft 1in	4.00m
Displacement	50,700lb	23,000kg
Sail area	8,826sqft	890m²
Designer	America¹ Design Team	
Builder	Eric Goetz, Bristol, Rhode Island	
Launched	1992	

Equation   page 149

This boat represented a jump up the ladder to a custom-built grand-prix boat by American yachtsman, Bill Alcott of St Claire Shores, Michigan. He didn't want to entirely leave behind his roots, a production J/44, so his brief to John Reichel and Jim Pugh was that he design a yacht of excellent aesthetics and one that was capable of "serious fast and fun time". He also wanted an ultra-competitive yacht for blasting around the Great Lakes and round the cans racing and he got what he wanted when *Equation* was the PHRF (Performance Handicap Rating Factor) winner of the 1995 Chicago–Mackinac race, the Great Lakes' biggest event.

Reichel/Pugh, who both served their time in Doug Peterson's

design studio in the 1970s before setting up their own practice in San Diego, have had a string of successful race boats, their most significant being *Abracadabra* and *Champosa*, winners of three International 50-foot class world championships in four years in the early 1990s. They were also members of Bill Koch's design team for the 1992 America's Cup winner *America¹* and *Morning Glory* which broke both the Cape–Rio and Sydney–Hobart course records in 1996.

Equation is a development of the previous *Morning Glory*, a 50-foot design for IMS racing and was built by Concordia Yachts. Besides her big Chicago–Mackinac win, she won the 1996 fourteen-boat Class 1 at Key West with six firsts and a second, and went on to race in the Caribbean and at Block Island.

LOA	50ft 3in	15.34m
LWL	42ft 7in	13.00m
Beam	14ft 2in	4.33m
Draught	10ft 6in	3.23m
Displacement	17,857lb	8,100kg
Sail area	1,926sqft	179m²
Designer	Reichel/Pugh	
Builder	Concordia Custom Yachts, Massachusetts	
Launched	1994	

Hunter's Child   pages 150–51

The string of shorthanded *Child* boats – first there was *Tuesday's Child*, followed by *Thursday's Child* and then *Hunter's Child* – stem from the board of Lars Bergstrom. All have been owned by Warren Luhrs, a father of eight, who, along with his brother John, has built a US$200million-turnover business. The family is from German immigrant stock which first settled in New Jersey, but Warren and John's father established the Luhrs boat-building name in Florida, a business joined by three others: Hunter (sailing yachts), Mainship and Silverton (motorboats).

Bergstrom, a meticulous flyer, was killed in a powered-glider accident in early 1997, a severe blow to Luhrs, long-standing friend and chief designer to Hunter. Luhrs' incredibly fertile mind was matched perfectly by Hunter's own receptiveness.

Aerodynamics were Bergstrom's main fascination but with partner Sven Ridder, they introduced significant ideas into the sailing. One was the Windex top-of-the-mast wind indicator. Another was the Bergstrom & Ridder backstayless rig, supported by swept back spreaders and counter-diagonals. He also worked with many famous designers. Dick Carter, for one, pioneering the NACA series 6 section foil for keels which became the

bedrock for keel design in the 1970s and '80s. Ron Holland used the alloy space frame to support the thin glassfibre skins on his seminal 40-footer, *Imp*.

Hunter's Child was built in England by Adrian Thompson and was characteristically full of innovation. The hull had a venturi-inducing hull slot underwater aimed at reducing friction. Like *Thursday's Child* her rudder was hinged on a gantry. This meant the blade was always vertical, even if the hull was well heeled, permitting a smaller than normal blade and lighter loading on the autopilot. Up forward a bowsprit on athwartships horns made handling gennakers easier for singlehanded sailing. The leeward horn could be used in very light winds to attach the gennaker, so opening up the all important slot between it and the mainsail. And spartan though the interior was, the entire navigation station, bunk and galley area was gimballed so that it remained horizontal. In solo sailing, a rested sailor is a faster one.

Luhrs' own plans to race the boat in the 1990–91 BOC solo round the world race fell through, but Steve Petengill took her to second place in the next BOC four years later.

LOA	60ft 0in	18.28m
LWL	59ft 0in	17.98m
Beam	16ft 0in	4.87m
Draught	14ft 0in	4.26m
Displacement	22,000lb	9,979kg
Sail area	1,924sqft	178.70m²
Designer	Hunter Design Group/ B & R Designs	
Builder	Paragon Composites, Totnes, England	
Launched	1990	

Boomerang   page 152

In the mid 1980s the maxi class, those yachts rating on or near the maximum 70.05 foot permitted under the IOR, reached its zenith. The yachts travelled globally competing in inshore series at places such as San Francisco, Honolulu (Hawaii), St Thomas (US Virgin Islands), Newport (Rhode Island), Nassau (Bahamas), Porto Cervo (Sardinia) and St Tropez, as well as the occasional offshore classics such at the Fastnet and Bermuda races.

Owned by New York-based shipping businessman George Coumantaros, *Boomerang* was designed by German Frers whose yachts dominated the maxi class in the 1980s. Rarely have there been racing machines which have been so elegant. Boomerang's colour scheme was classically simple – a blue/black hull, with white decks and bottom above and below, picked out by red boot top and a gold cove line – and skipper Jeff Neuberth ensured she never looked less than immaculate.

Ironically *Boomerang*'s success was trumped by subsequent Frers sisterships fitted with fractional rigs, most notably Raul Gardini's *Il Moro di Venezia* from Italy, and then by Bill Koch's new *Matador²*, the result of a ten-year tank-test and VPP (Velocity Prediction Program) development programme, which was so successful that she stifled the class.

LOA	80ft 6in	24.56m
LWL	66ft 3in	20.20m
Beam	19ft 7in	6.00m
Draught	12ft 6in	3.85m
Displacement	80,279lb	35,000kg
Sail area	4,007sqft	372.32m²
Designer	German Frers Jr	
Builder	Robert E. Derecktor, New York	
Launched	1984	

Flash Gordon 3 page 153
and Numbers

One of the great battles of the 1997 Champagne Mumm Admiral's Cup was amongst the big IMS boats, notably *Flash Gordon 3* and *Numbers*. *Flash* was built in New Zealand for Helmut Jahn, the Chicago architect who designed the United Airlines terminal at O'Hare airport, the James R. Thompson Centre in Chicago Loop and the Messa Turn, until recently Berlin's tallest building – and a place in the US team. Her deadliest rival was *Numbers*, sailing for New Zealand, but actually a Canadian boat, belonging to John Risley of Nova Scotia.

Numbers was launched first, right at the end of 1996. By offering her to the Kiwis, it enabled New Zealand to return to the Admiral's Cup after a four-year gap. For skipper Russell Coutts, it allowed him to bring half his America's Cup-winning Team New Zealand aboard as part of his strategy for defending the America's Cup in 2000. Wherever there was a hot class or event, Coutts wanted TNZ sailors to be involved. Throughout the Admiral's Cup Coutts harried *Flash Gordon 3* around every start zone, effectively match racing his American rival. At the back of *Flash* were Ken Read and Jim Brady, two exceptionally talented Americans. Read has won more J/24 World Championships than anyone else. Brady, like Coutts, is an Olympic gold medallist.

Flash was launched in early June and was Bruce Farr's latest thinking for an IMS 49-footer. Unsurprisingly, she got better as the Admiral's Cup went on and became top boat of the series, doing well in the long Channel and Fastnet Race which score extra points. A bad Fastnet for *Numbers*, in which she fell out of the wind on the first night off Portland Bill and never got back into the hunt, sealed a poor series for the Kiwis. They had been favourites to win the Cup but weren't even close in the end.

Numbers was designed by Jim Taylor and Penn Edmunds, best known for designing *Matador²* and *America³* for Bill Koch, and utilized the design tools from both the *America³* and Team New Zealand America's Cup campaigns. In a class where variations are subtle, *Numbers* was original in many areas. Her hull was longer and narrower than the Farr type. Her keel carried no bulb. She was built in a sophisticated way from Kevlar to be as light and stiff as carbon fibre but without the rating penalty. What caught the eye the most was her clever carbon fibre spar, large in section but very thin walled. To prevent buckling when it was hauled forward for downwind sailing, it was made from two overlapping sections which allowed it to hinge towards the bow by a dramatic amount. Needless to say, the Americans tried protesting the spar out of the competition, without success, but it summed up the intensity of the duel between *Numbers* and *Flash Gordon 3*.

Numbers

LOA	49ft 2in	15.00m
LWL	43ft 7in	13.30m
Beam	11ft 7in	3.53m
Draught	9ft 10in	3.00m
Displacement	20,350lb	9,250kg
Sail area	1,369sqft	127.30m²
Designer	Jim Taylor & Penn Edmunds Associates	
Builder	Goetz Boatworks, Bristol, Rhode Island	
Launched	1996	

Flash Gordon 3

LOA	49ft 4in	15.03m
LWL	42ft 6in	12.96m
Beam	14ft 2in	4.32m
Draught	11ft 0in	3.34m
Displacement	19,642lb	8,928kg
Sail area	1,711sqft	159m²
Designer	Bruce Farr & Associates	
Builder	Cookson Boats, Auckland	
Launched	1997	

Bimblegumbie/Ninety-Seven pages 154–5

Andrew Strachan's mid-blue *Ninety-Seven* was one of the early grand-prix race boats designed once the administrators of off-shore racing had decided that the IMS rule was successor to the IOR at elite level.

At 46 feet, designer Bruce Farr positioned the boat midway between the new ILC40 class and the faster, bigger IMS 50-footers. It was a practical proposition since it was known in 1993 that there was going to be a ILC46 class slotted in above the ILC40s for boats with an overall length of around 45–7 feet and in mixed fleets, a 46-footer is a nice size: large enough to power away from the melée of smaller yachts and into clear air without having to compete directly with the more powerful 50-footers.

Ninety-Seven was built at a time when carbon fibre was still off the menu for IMS in 1993 and even when it was permitted for the 1994 season, it carried a significant rating penalty. The boat saw active service, winning her class in the 1994 Sydney–Hobart race, competing in the Pacific at the Kenwood Cup, being chartered by Britain for the 1995 Southern Cross series in Sydney and then being chartered by Keith Jacobs of Hong Kong, who named her after his own string of race boats – *Bimblegumbie* – for the 1995 Champagne Mumm Admiral's Cup.

LOA	46ft 8in	14.27m
LWL	40ft 5in	12.36m
Beam	14ft 1in	4.31m
Draught	9ft 3in	2.85m
Displacement	18,342lb	8,320kg
Sail area	1,454sqft	135m²
Designer	Bruce Farr & Associates	
Builder	Boat Speed, Australia	
Launched	1993	

La Poste pages 156–7

This has to go down as one of the more imaginative sponsorships in sailing for the French post office, not once, but twice, brought their distinctive yellow and blue colours to the Whitbread race. Under the leadership of Daniel Malle from the Nantes post office, *La Poste* was a plucky entry in the 1989–90 Whitbread, a perennial back marker in a small production racer, a Beneteau First 51. Just completing the course was a success.

But they came back in the 1993–4 as contenders, in a brand-new Bruce Farr-designed maxi which was built in a collaborative effort with Pierre Fehlmann's Swiss entry, *Merit Cup*. Compared with Grant Dalton's *New Zealand Endeavour*, which went on to win the maxi division, *La Poste* and *Merit Cup* were shorter,

heavier and had more sail area. The boats were built by Decision SA of Switzerland, with input from Bénéteau. Having bought into the best technology, Malle made sure he was up to speed on the racing side, employing coaches from the French National Sailing School and having America's Cup helmsman Marc Bouet and Olympic 470 gold medallist Luc Pillot aboard during their work-up in the Round Europe Race some three months before the Whitbread start. His crew still counted postal workers amongst its ranks but now also Admiral's Cup and multihull professionals such as Benoit Caignaert, Michel Desjoyeaux and Dominique Conin.

Reaching the first leg stop over in Punta del Este, Uruguay, some 19 hours behind *Merit Cup* set the tone for the race. Twenty-one different sailors ended up crewing on the boat as personnel came and went: only seven sailed all six legs. France's biggest sailing hero, Eric Tabarly, was brought in to take over the boat for the last four legs but the gloss never came. Structural problems whilst beating up the Brazilian coast from Punta del Este to Fort Lauderdale added to the woes. *La Poste* eventually finished third out of four maxis and was seventh fastest around the world in a fleet of 14.

LOA	84ft 9in	25.90m
LWL	65ft 3in	19.92m
Beam	19ft 2in	5.85m
Draught	12ft 8in	3.90m
Displacement	64,951lb	29,462kg
Sail area	4,205sqft	390.80m²
Designer	Bruce Farr & Associates	
Builder	Decision SA, Switzerland	
Launched	1993	

Brava Q8 pages 158–9

For much of the late 1980s and first half of the 90s, Italy's Champagne Mumm Admiral's Cup teams have been run less like a nationally selected squad and more like an owner's collective with Pasquale Landolfi as its driving force. He missed involvement in only two Italian teams from 1981 until their eventual triumph in 1995 when Italy won for the time in 35 years of trying. Fittingly Landolfi's *Brava Q8* was the top yacht of the series.

Pasquale Landolfi has made this 40-foot grand-prix offshore boat his own, his record in the One Ton Cup and ILC40 class since 1987 being second to none. Winning the Admiral's Cup came in Pasquale Landolfi's 68th year and a more committed owner would be hard to find. Few sail offshore in their boats nowadays as modern grand-prix boats tend to be somewhat inhospitable below, though that is not the objection. Rather it is the overriding requirement to act as live ballast, hiking hard on the gunwale. Landolfi is a one time water polo player and has lost none of his competitiveness. The Italians had contrived to lose the Cup in 1993 and trailed the US team into the 1995 Fastnet, yet sensing a come from behind victory could be theirs, Landolfi hiked for the last 22 hours of the five days to ensure a win for his team, individual honours for *Brava Q8* amongst the Admiral's Cupper and second overall in the entire Fastnet fleet.

LOA	41ft 0in	12.50m
LWL	36ft 3in	11.08m
Beam	13ft 0in	3.97m
Draught	8ft 5in	2.59m
Displacement	13,306lb	6,036kg
Sail area	1,277sqft	118.60m²
Designer	Bruce Farr & Associates	
Builder	Cookson Boatbuilders, Auckland	
Launched	1995	

Apricot/Exide Challenger page 160

It's not often that a yacht is famous for the underside of her hull, but in early January 1997 TV viewers across the world were treated to a dramatic rescue deep in the Southern Ocean of British solo sailor Tony Bullimore.

His 60-foot wing-master schooner was racing in the Vendée Globe solo, non-stop round the world race (renamed *Exide Challenger* after receiving sponsorship from the battery manufacturer just before the start in November) from the French fishing port of Les Sables d'Olonne, when the second big blow since entering the Southern Ocean came through. Winds rose from 25 to 35 to 45 to 55 knots. Bullimore had everything lashed down, and *Exide Challenger* running under her bare wing masts when – bang – the keel snapped off. The yacht rolled onto the deck and Bullimore found himself standing on the deckhead. He spent the first night like that, until a deck house window broke. "Water starting coming in like the Niagara Falls," said Bullimore in what turned into an epic survival effort. His plight was perilous: 1,500 miles from Australia and 900 miles from Antarctica.

Until the Royal Australian Navy's frigate *HMAS Adelaide* got to him three days later, and launched an inflatable with a crew of divers, no one knew if Bullimore was dead or alive. When divers banged on the hull side they were greeted by knocking from inside. Taking three deep breaths, Bullimore swam out from his sanctuary inside, where in a dry suit and on a bunk, he managed to stay mostly out of the water. Bullimore's plight and rescue made headlines worldwide and his rescue was covered by TV. The keel's loss has not been explained, though one possible reason could have been adding extra weight to it. The boat's respected original designers were Martyn Smith, a senior structural engineer with British Aerospace, and Barry Noble, who also created Bullimore's previous yacht, the 60-foot trimaran *Spirit of Apricot*.

LOA	60ft 0in	18.29m
LWL	59ft 0in	18.00m
Beam	16ft 0in	4.88m
Draught	13ft 4in	4.15m
Displacement	21,604lb	9,800kg
Sail area	2,400sqft	222.90m²
Designer	Noble Smith Designs	
Builder	Rocknes Court, Bristol	
Launched	1993	

ENZA page 161

Whatever they say, you can compare apples and pears. In this case it is the 92-foot catamaran *ENZA* and what she achieved in her former life as *TAG Heuer* and what she went on to do later in setting a new round the world record, beating *Commodore Explorer*'s time to become the second holder of the Jules Verne Trophée after her successful circumnavigation by sailing knights, Sir Peter Blake and Sir Robin Knox-Johnston.

With multihulls, you have to recalibrate your ideas of "big". *ENZA* is tennis-court big at 92 feet long by 45 feet wide. She's fast too. Thirty knots fast, the sort of speed a highly powered motorboat is capable of. Looking aft from on board while the boat is at full chat is like watching a hydro dam sluice gate. She was built in Canada in 1982 by Canadair and was one of the very first large carbon fibre, pre-impregnated structures, then common place in the aerospace industry on smaller scales but largely untested in yacht use. She was designed by feted Briton Nigel Irens, who had prospered in the intensely competitive French market, for Canadian skipper Mike Birch. Sponsored by the Saudi/Swiss company TAG Heuer and raced in the Quebec–St Malo race

amongst others. It was the fertile French sailing scene which threw up the idea of the Jules Verne Trophée: a dash around the planet to see if Phileas Fogg's fictional 80-day circumnavigation could be bettered in fact. At the time, the quickest anyone had sailed around the world was the 104 days taken by Titouan Lamazou, inevitably a Frenchman in a French race, the Globe Challenge. He sailed solo in a 60-foot monohull, so a fully crewed multi could easily better it, but by how much?

The answer came in 1993 when Bruno Peyron and four crew aboard *Commodore Explorer* set a time from Ushant (France's north-west corner) to Ushant of 79 days 6 hours 15 minutes. *ENZA*, named after Blake's sponsors the New Zealand Apple & Pear Marketing board, made an attempt that same winter but pulled out south of Cape Town when a floating object punched a hole in one hull. *ENZA* stuck by Blake and Knox-Johnston for another attempt 12 months later. In the intervening period, crew member David Alan-Williams modified the boat, putting more buoyancy in the bows and extending the sterns to stretch the boat from 85 feet to 92 feet. The Apples & Pears boat was triumphant, bettering *Commodore Explorer*'s time by more than four days with a record of 74 days 22 hours 17 minutes, a time which stood until 1997 when Olivier der Kersauson's *Sport-Elec* posted a time of 71 days 14 hours 18 minutes.

ENZA, renamed *Royal & Sun Alliance*, is now owned by Tracy Edwards, intent on making an all-women's assault on the Jules Verne Trophée.

LOA	92ft 0in	28.04m
LWL	85ft 0in	25.90m
Beam	42ft 0in	12.80m
Draught	2ft 5in	0.76m
Displacement	21,840lb	9,750kg
Sail area	3,832sqft	356m²
Designer	Nigel Irens & David Alan-Williams	
Builder	Canadair	
Launched	1982	

Infinity page 162

Green topsides and an evergreen performance has kept John Thomson's yacht at the head of the IMS big boat fleet since her launch in 1993. Her results tally is all the more commendable given that Thomson is a Corinthian owner who drives his own yacht at the highest level and that *Infinity* has had relatively little in the way of modifications.

For the 1996 season she was updated with a new keel and rudder but the biggest change came for the 1997 season when a new carbon fibre mast was stepped. *Infinity* won from the word go and she has rarely failed to post a top three finish in any series she has sailed. Her first big win was in IMS Class A at the 1994 Key West Race Week, something she repeated a year later in 1995. She also won the SORC regatta at Miami in 1994 but her crew rate their 1996 Kenwood Cup win Hawaii as the one to savour. Always immaculately turned out, Thomson has often had North Sails' president Tom Whidden as his tactician, a job he does routinely for Dennis Conner in the America's Cup, with Gould "Stretch" Ryder as the regular navigator. Designer Bruce Nelson, also an exceptionally talented sailor, has also been a frequent crew member.

LOA	49ft 7in	15.10m
LWL	40ft 6in	12.30m
Beam	14ft 0in	4.26m
Draught	9ft 8in	3.00m
Displacement	20,300lb	9,208kg
Sail area	1,440sqft	134m²
Designer	Nelson/Marek Yacht Design	
Builder	Cookson Boats, Auckland	
Launched	1993	

Wizard page 163

Andrew Louw commissioned this 56-footer from Alex Simonis, requiring a fast racer-cruiser. She was launched in November 1991 to allow good time to optimize the boat for the following Cape–Rio race and before she left, *Wizard* raced in South Africa's principal big boat series, Rothmans Week, taking line honours in all races and finishing second overall on corrected time. She started the Cape–Rio race well, but finished fifth overall as the larger yachts got away, leaving the smaller boats stuck in lighter winds.

Initially *Wizard* was done little favour by the IMS rule's harsh treatment of light displacement yachts, which was relaxed from 1994 onwards. Andrew Louw has always kept *Wizard* optimized to the rule and his yachts have built up a steady reputation for taking line honours and showing well on handicap. Five years after her launch she was first boat home and corrected time winner in the 1997 Vasco da Gama 265-miler.

Wizard set a course record in the 1995 Double Cape race, which makes two laps of the South African coast between Cape Town and Cape of Good Hope, and scored another fifth in the 1996 Cape–Rio race, after which she went to race at Antigua Sailing Week, winning three out of five races in class.

LOA	55ft 9in	17.03m
LWL	51ft 4in	15.67m
Beam	16ft 9in	5.15m
Draught	10ft 3in	3.15m
Displacement	27,550lb	12,500kg
Sail area	2,045sqft	190m²
Designer	Alexander Simonis	
Builder	J. M. Boatbuilders, Cape Town	
Launched	1991	

Coyote page 164–5

A yacht tinged with tragedy, *Coyote* never managed to compete in the race she was commissioned for, the Vendée Globe non-stop solo round the world, as the man who planned to race her was lost in the Atlantic delivering the Open 60 class yacht from New York to the start line in Les Sables d'Olonne.

All those attending the November 1992 start in the fishing port north of Bordeaux will remember the anxious wait for news, good news, about American Mike Plant. It never came. Instead the capsized *Coyote* was eventually found drifting, the lead bulb snapped off her deep, slender keel. Of Plant there was no sign.

Plant had won the 50-foot class in the BOC solo, four-stage round the world race two years before and much was expected of him and his beamy, powerful Rodger Martin-designed yacht. His fiancée Helen Davis organized the salvage of the yacht of which she was co-owner in early 1993 and a multi-million dollar lawsuit she brought against the builder was settled out of court.

It was a moment of real emotion when *Coyote* left Charleston, South Carolina, for the next BOC in 1994–5, this time in the hands of another American, David Scully, who finished fifth. Since then, she has been chartered by Briton Josh Hall, who, raced Plant's earlier 50-foot Martin-designed boat *Airco Distributor* as *Spirit of Ipswich*, and his sailing partner Bob Hooke. Hall was first to finish in the 1995 Bermuda One-Two and came a highly commendable second to Yves Parlier's radical *Aquitaine Innovations*, in the 60ft monohull class of the 1996 Europe-1 Singlehanded Transatlantic.

Even familiarity gained since the Open 60s' appearance in the early 1990s has not lessened their extreme look: *Coyote*'s beam is one third of her length to give the internal water ballast tanks maximum righting leverage and the rig piles on more sail area than fully crewed grand-prix yacht of the same length would ever carry.

LOA	60ft 0in	18.28m
LWL	57ft 0in	17.37m
Beam	19ft 4in	5.89m
Draught	14ft 0in	4.26m
Displacement	21,500lb	9,752kg
Sail area	2,895sqft	269m²
Designer	Rodger Martin Yacht Design	
Builder	Concordia Custom Yachts	
Launched	1992	

Whitbread Race pages 166–7

The Solent has seen some spectacular send-offs but the seventh Whitbread race start from the Royal Yacht Squadron in Cowes on 29 September 1997 was special. It was only the second time that the Whitbread fleet has headed out west through the narrows at Hurst Castle rather than leave the Solent eastabouts via Spithead. A great day and a fitting way for Whitbread to bow out of their sponsorship after 25 years and pass the race on to Volvo of Sweden.

As such it was like popping the cork from a bottle: there might have been only ten yachts racing, but they sat up under spinnakers and moved effortlessly along at 14–15 knots in the 20 knot southerly breeze, which meant that the 2–3,000 spectator boats were breathless in keeping up. They whipped the Solent into meringue-like peaks, standing waves 5 feet high and the surface

turned white by the boiling water. The RAF's Red Arrows had made one of their thunderously balletic displays minutes before the start, setting the tone for the charge that was to follow.

1997–8 was the second time that the Whitbread 60 class had been used. When they had raced four years before with IOR 83-foot maxis, the race organisers deliberately tied one hand behind the W60s' back for fear that their speed might show up the longer boats. Second time out, the W60s were unshackled, liberated to fly tennis-court size spinnakers from the masthead instead of merely from the hounds. In light to moderate winds, this extra sail brought noticeable gains. In stronger winds, the extra performance comes much from sweeter hull shapes which are easier to drive harder, than more horsepower. Even so, Dennis Conner's *Toshiba* set a new monohull world record of 424 miles in 24 hours during her transatlantic delivery before the start, adding some 10 miles to the previous record set by Lawrie Smith's *Intrum Justitia* in the previous Whitbread.

Eight of the ten entries all come from New Zealand designer Bruce Farr with seven of the fleet shown here: *EF Language* (Paul Cayard), *Innovation Kvaerner* (Knut Frostad), *Toshiba* (Chris Dickson), *EF Education* (Christine Guillou), *Merit Cup* (Grant Dalton), *America's Challenge* (Ross Field) and *Chessie Racing* (George Collins).

LOA	64ft 0in	19.50m
LWL	56ft 8in	17.28m
Beam	17ft 2in	5.25m
Draught	12ft 4in	3.75m
Displacement	29,700lb	13,500kg
Sail area	2,153sqft	200m²

Ville de Cherbourg pages 168–9

"She was like a comet," says Halvard Mabire of his red 60-footer's brief life, "shining bright, but gone almost as soon as she had arrived." Launched for the 1993 season, she won the Open 60 monohull class in the Round Europe Race, the 60ft Class 1 in the 1994 Europe 1 Twostar Transatlantic Race from Plymouth to Newport and was lost a few months later in the early stages of the Route du Rhum race from St Malo.

Mabire lost everything save his life, for sponsorship was late coming to the project, which was run on the tightest of budgets, and the boat was uninsured. Mabire is one of France's great can-do sailors, skilled in so many areas and he had built *Ville de Cherbourg* himself. He attests that his yacht sank because of a problem with the only part he had not built, the steel fin for the keel which suffered alleged welding failure. Interestingly, *Ville de Cherbourg* was built in rented space alongside Isabelle Autissier's own Open 60, *Ecureuil Poiteau Charentes* at Marc Pinta's yard, and *Ville de Cherbourg* beat her in the Round Europe Race, but when Autissier was forced to abandon her first attempt on the New York–San Francisco record, it was due to a welding problem on her canting keel and the same metal fabricator was involved. *Ville de Cherbourg* was three days out of St Malo, some 500 miles west of Brest, when Mabire heard a bang in the night. Suspecting a sheared keel bolt he was returning to Brest when, the next day, his boat suddenly capsized. Some two hours in the water and another 12 on the upturned hull gave him ample time to study where the fin had snapped off. But his luck was in. Beyond helicopter range, the Royal Navy fleet auxiliary *Bramble Leaf* was 70 miles away when his Mayday went out and the ship diverted, her crew rescuing Mabire in a rigid inflatable, probably about the only means by which he could be recovered.

He ended up in Cornwall. "After rescue by the inflatable, transfer by ship and then helicopter before returning to France by light aircraft, Mabire joked: "the only things I did not do the Rhum race in were a balloon and train!"

Ville de Cherbourg was a development of the Joubert/Nivelt-designed *Charente Maritime*, with shape about the only common factor. Mabire's boat was lighter and more powerful. She weighed 2.5 tons lighter at 8.5 tons, had a lighter, deeper keel and more sail area carried on the tallest mast seen on an Open 60 at 26 metres high. Mabire and colleagues had made the mast mould themselves and created a carbon fibre spar which, fully dressed with all fittings, weighed just 348kg. She had such power that the first reef went in at 12 knots windspeed. Not for nothing was she so fast, so briefly.

LOA	60ft 0in	18.28m
LWL	57ft 3in	17.50m
Beam	17ft 1in	5.20m
Draught	14ft 7in	4.50m
Displacement	19,040lb	8,600kg
Sail area	2,798sqft	270m²
Designer	Joubert/Nivelt, Mabire & de Rivogre	
Builder	Halvard Mabire & Christine Guillou c/o Marc Pinta	
Launched	1993	

Milene V page 170

The sheer cost of building and running a racing maxi means that young owners are a rarity. Albert Mirlesse was among the oldest. In 1990, when the old-style IOR maxis were in their penultimate season before the class went quiet before a rebirth in 1995 with IMS boats, the French owner of *Milene V* was racing hard aged 75. "I don't feel the strain too much!" he said.

In fact Mirlesse loved his racing. He came to it early and late in his life, starting in 1932. Then after fighting for the Free French in World War II and then going on to become an industrial consultant in France and the developing countries, he bought his first yacht in 1970. Competing in the Fastnet Race of 1971 fuelled the competitive juices and he eventually owned a stable of three Swan yachts, 48, 47 and 441, competed in the Admiral's Cup at Cowes three times and then moved up the maxi class following a convivial discussion with Baron Edmund de Rothschild.

Milene V was the only French-designed maxi in a class dominated by Ron Holland, German Frers and Bruce Farr, created by Gilles Vaton, best known for his low-slung, sporty high-performance cruisers. She was also fractionally rigged, long before *Il Moro di Venezia III* established this as the the rig to win with. *Milene V*'s results were rarely at the top of the table and Mirlesse chose not to have his crews brimful of professionals. "The atmosphere on board is very relaxed and we really consider ourselves amateurs," he explained at the time. Friendship and fun were, it seems, more important than trophies.

LOA	80ft 1in	24.48m
LWL	64ft 8in	19.75m
Beam	20ft 3in	6.20m
Draught	13ft 8in	4.20m
Displacement	73,832lb	33,490kg
Sail area	3,661sqft	340m²
Designer	Gilles Vaton	
Builder	Constructions Mechanique de Normandie, Cherbourg	
Launched	1985	

Tokio page 171

It was during New Zealand's first ever America's Cup challenge, in 1987 in Fremantle, that Chris Dickson was dubbed "a choir boy with the eyes of a U-boat commander", which summed up to a tee his intensely competitive spirit lurking inside a cherubic frame.

Everyone inside the sport has their view of Dickson now. A feisty personality, he refuses to be ignored. Intelligent, abrasive, articulate, combative, enigmatic, mercurial, astute, obnoxious and so on: Dickson has been labelled with them all. Perhaps more than any other competitor in sailing, Dennis Conner included, Dickson encapsulates the tussle between genius and caprice that is the hallmark of many sportsmen in other fields.

From triple world championships as a youth, Dickson moved seamlessly into big boats, often seen steering the Frers 45 *Scaramouche*, when not yet turned 20, before winning his place at the wheel of *KZ–7* in Fremantle as a 25-year old and taking her to an unprecedented 38:1 win:lose record in the challenger trials before being knocked out by Dennis Conner.

Dickson went on to win three world match racing titles before becoming a hired gun for Japan's first ever America's Cup challenge in 1992 at San Diego. Despite huge frustrations, Dickson got his yacht to the challenger semi-finals. He surprised everyone with his debut in the 1993–4 Whitbread race having shown little inclination towards marathon ocean racing. Dickson, of course, did not see it as such. To him, as a high earning professional, this was the second biggest event outside of the America's Cup so he needed to be part it and he brought his particular brand of intensity to it, which nearly resulted in a debut victory.

This was only thwarted by dismasting on the fifth leg from Punta del Este in Uruguay to Fort Lauderdale. Dickson was beating into a 30-knot headwind and a very awkward sea. All the water ballast tanks were full but as far as his rivals were concerned, there were two further contributory factors: Dickson had put on a light inshore mainsail for the leg, which was way too full and powerful for the conditions; and his quest to run his campaign on the tightest of budgets meant that he did not replace rigging components during the stopovers as others had done.

Whatever, Dickson's instinctive feel for his boat's speeds and his constant pressure on the crew to keep it at 100 per cent set new standards in the Whitbread. And his helming on the last leg, when *Tokio* carried a spinnaker by the lee past the Scillies and The Lizard even had his grizzled crew speechless at Dickson's virtuosity.

The name *Tokio*? Dickson had used his Japanese connections with the giant Dentsu advertising agency who had underwritten his two boat campaign in the anticipation of sponsors coming aboard. Curiously none did, but Dickson's campaign was secure. His second boat, a wild card John Swarbrick design, did not show well in testing against the Bruce Farr yacht Dickson then raced with such verve.

LOA	63ft 9in	19.50m
LWL	56ft 6in	17.24m
Beam	17ft 1in	5.24m
Draught	12ft 2in	3.74m
Displacement	29,453lb	13,360kg
Sail area	2,762sqft	256.60m²
Designer	Bruce Farr & Associates	
Builder	Cookson Boats, Auckland	
Launched	1993	

Pinta page 172

Among the long line of *Pintas* owned by German Willi Illbruck, each with their distinctive green lettering on the topsides, the 1995 ILC46 yacht remains a favourite. She won the inaugural ILC46 World Championships that year, was successful in the Sardinia Cup in Porto Cervo and was, in her crews' eyes, a great yacht to sail.

Willi Illbruck entered mainstream international competition with a Doug Peterson-designed yacht, the ex-*Yena*, but from 1982 onwards has remained faithful to the Judel/Vrolijk design partnership for all his subsequent yachts bar one, two of them being part of the winning German Admiral's Cup teams of 1983 and 1993. The Judel/Vrolijk alliance was formed over a beer when Rolk Vrolijk, then working for Canadian designers C&C, met Friedrich Judel in a bar in Kiel, the centre of German sailing. Judel had studied shipbuilding in Bremen but was bemoaning the lack of time to complete his design for a Mini Ton yacht. Joining forces, they produced the *Popcorn* Mini Tonner and *Quadriga* Quarter Tonner before breaking through with the 1981 minimum rating Admiral's Cup yacht *Düsselboot* which really put them on the map.

She caught Willi Illbruck's eye and his newest yacht, *Pinta Smeralda*, is a 70-foot express cruiser, also from Judel/Vrolijk.

LOA	47ft 5in	14.50mm
LWL	40ft 0in	12.35m
Beam	14ft 8in	4.54m
Draught	7ft 8in	2.40m
Displacement	17,857lb	8,100kg
Sail area	1,302sqft	121m²
Designer	Judel/Vrolijk	
Builder	Marten Marine, Auckland	
Launched	1995	

Titan page 173

While the IMS put down roots as the grand-prix rule in the early to mid 1990s, the number of custom-built boats was relatively small, yet the number of the series produced ones were increasing as owners preferred the lower risks associated with a production boat. American Barry Carroll was in the forefront of this market from his yard in Bristol, Rhode Island, with designs from Bill

Tripp, Bruce Nelson and Bruce Farr. *Titan* was one of the most successful of the Nelson/Marek 46s, aimed at both open IMS handicap racing and to the fit parameters of the ILC46 (International Level Class) class where all the boats race on a common rating.

Titan may have been a series-built yacht but was in all other respects a flat-out race boat. Her parameters of length, displacement, beam and sail area were studied by the Nelson/Marek's office Velocity Prediction Programs. The hull is fine forward with a low resistance shape, which gains stability and sailing length as it heels. The rig is powerful to give dinghy like acceleration. Launched in January 1995 she had a great debut season, third in class at Key West followed up by firsts at SORC, Antigua Sailing Week and Block Island Race week, interspersed by a charter to David Horwitz for South Africa's Champagne Mumm Admiral's Cup team where as *Sansui Challenger* she won two inshore races in the eight-boat ILC46 class. Since then, *Titan* has sailed under Puerto Rican colours on the Caribbean circuit.

LOA	46ft 6in	14.20m
LWL	36ft 7in	11.20m
Beam	13ft 6in	4.14m
Draught	9ft 1in	2.77m
Displacement	18,100lb	8,210kg
Sail area	1,173sqft	108.90m²
Designer	Nelson/Marek Yacht Design	
Builder	Carroll Marine, Bristol, Rhode Island	
Launched	1995	

Lakota page 174

Lakota, named after a native American Indian tribe, was launched as *Pierre 1ᵉʳ* for France's Florence Arthaud, before she was taken over by Chicago futures-commodity broker Steve Fossett. Record-breaking is Fossett's forte and not just at sea, but in *Lakota* he has established seven new sailing records: Round Ireland nonstop, Round the Isle of Wight, Round Britain & Ireland non-stop, Honolulu–Yokohama and each way on the Yokohama–San Francisco. This last one reveals much about the man, for having set the fully crewed record for Yokohama–San Francisco in 1995, he went back a year later to do it again on his own. He took nearly three and half days longer but was still three days better than the previous solo record. *Lakota* was designed by the French partnership of Marc van Peteghem and Vincent Lauriot Prévost, famous for the Formula 40 *Biscuits Cantreau*, Laurent Bourgnon's *RMO/Primagaz* and Olivier de Kersauson's *Poulain/Charal/Lyonnaise des Eaux/Sport Elec* which set the world's fastest circumnavigation in 1997. Two sisterships of *Pierre 1ᵉʳ Lakota* were built for Kevin Costner's *Waterworld* movie.

Lakota's American owner made the headlines in 1997 when he attempted to balloon around the world non-stop, at the same time as Richard Branson's crew and a Swiss team. Fossett got the furthest in the smallest, most modest balloon and on his own. Twelve hours lost in negotiating permission to fly through Libyan airspace cost too much fuel, so Fossett abandoned the attempt in India, though not before setting distance and endurance records of 5,435 miles and 6 days 10 hours 0 minutes.

Fossett is the man who failed to make his school running, cross country and swimming teams but, who as an adult ran the Boston marathon, swam the English Channel and posted a sub-30 hour time in the Leadville 100-mile trek in Colorado. He has also raced at Le Mans, competed in the Paris–Dakar rally, finished the brutal Iditarod dog-sled race in Alaska and climbed the highest peaks in Alaska, Argentina, Kenya and Antarctica. You might say that only Everest awaits him but, in a rare failure, he has tried that already.

LOA	60ft 0in	18.28m
LWL	60ft 0in	18.28m
Beam	50ft 0in	15.24m
Draught	13ft 0in	3.96m
Displacement	13,440lb	6,096kg
Sail area	3,046sqft	283m²
Designer	Marc van Peteghem &	
	Vincent Lauriot Prévost	
Builder	CDK Composites, France	
Launched	1992	

Rubin XII page 175

With his first appearance in 1963, Hans-Otto Schumann has a strong claim to be longest serving Admiral's Cup competitor, enjoying a two-year lead on Australian Syd Fischer of *Ragamuffin* fame. Hans-Otto Schuman's own yachts are a familiar part of the scenery and not just because of the *Rubin* name: he has stuck to the same white topsides and wide red-boot top for four decades. Hans-Otto Schumann has also long held a fascination with the science of sailing. In the 1960s he experimented with quilted

spinnakers to explore venturi effects; in the 1970s he tank tested his Sparkman & Stephens yacht when that design office was at its peak and altered the stern; in the 1980s he was one of the first to move away from trapezoidal keel shapes and try-out a shark's fin configuration on his Judel/Vrolijk One-Tonner. Several times he has put new hulls under the deck of the previous *Rubin* to limit the cost of producing an entirely new hull.

LOA	44ft 1in	13.44m
LWL	37ft 7in	11.50m
Beam	13ft 5in	4.12m
Draught	8ft 6in	2.63m
Displacement	17,923lb	8,130kg
Sail area	1,130sqft	105m²
Designer	Judel & Vrolijk	
Builder	Schutzwerke/Yachtwerft Wedel	
Launched	1991	

Stars & Stripes page 176

This is the boat which returned the America's Cup to the USA after a brief three-year stay in Australia: having lost the Cup to Alan Bond's *Australia II* off Newport in September 1983, Dennis Conner won it back at Fremantle in February 1987.

Ironically it was a boat Conner felt he did not need, one his Sail America syndicate could not really justify, but ultimately she was needed, for hindsight showed that if Conner had stuck with preferred *Stars & Stripes '85*, he would not have made the challenger finals. As he had done with his intensive two-boat campaign of 1980, when the hours he sailed *Enterprise* and *Freedom* would have been enough to go around the world, so Conner attempted a four-boat campaign in 1987, or five, if you count the defeated 1983 defender *Liberty*. Conner used his 1983 discarded boats, *Magic* and *Spirit*, to bracket the length v displacement choice, sinking the light and short *Magic* down and lightening the long, heavy *Spirit*.

His design team numbered 20 with John Marshall its ring master and Brit Chance, David Pedrick and Bruce Nelson, the principal designers. They ran thousands of Velocity Prediction Programs, hundreds of computational fluid dynamics flow codes and no fewer than 33 one third scale models in the test tank, roping in expertise from Science Applications International and Grumman Aerospace.

What set *Stars & Stripes '87* apart was the search for minimum rating length under the 12-metre rule, maximum effective sailing length and superior wave making characteristics. This results in a pronounced chin on her forward waterline and rather ugly square, flat sections aft. The result was stupendously effective. She was

never an easy boat to sail, and throughout three months of trials, the mast position was altered, a deeper rudder fitted, flatter sail shapes tried and smaller delta wings fitted until *Stars & Stripes* reached her potential.

She stopped the hitherto all-conquering New Zealanders' *KZ–7* in her tracks in the challenger final and brushed aside the Australian defender *Kookaburra III* effortlessly. Conner was back in the business and the Cup back in American hands, until 1995 at least, and the Kiwis' successful third try. When Derecktor's yard in Newport, Rhode Island started cutting metal at the end of March 1986, *Stars & Stripes '87* was the last 12-metre ever built for the Cup as the much bigger International America's Cup Class replaced the Twelves for the 1992 series.

LOA	64ft 3in	19.59m
LWL	44ft 6in	13.59m
Beam	12ft 6in	3.81m
Draught	8ft 0in	2.44m
Displacement	63,974lb	29,000kg
Sail area	1,750sqft	162.75m²
Designer	Chance, Pedrick & Nelson	
Builder	Derecktor, Mamaronek, Rhode Island	
Launched	1986	

Glossary of Terms, Races and Rules

AMERICA'S CUP

The longest running international event in sport. Named after the yacht *America*, brought to the UK by a New York syndicate for the Great Exhibition. She trounced the best UK yachts in a race around the Isle of Wight and the cup she won was donated for "friendly competition between nations". Only twice has a challenger beaten the US defender, the Australians in 1983 and the New Zealanders in 1995.

ADMIRAL'S CUP

Nowadays the Champagne Mumm Admiral's Cup, but originally created in 1957 by British yachtsmen, among them the Admiral of the Royal Ocean Racing Club, Buster de Guingand, to encourage overseas yachts to come to England for Cowes Week. It developed in its own right and in the 1970s and early '80s was the single most influential offshore racing event in the world. It retains its three boats per nation format, mixing inshore with offshore racing and is run in odd numbered years.

ARC

Atlantic Rally for Cruisers – an annual event attracting between 125 and 250 yachts for the crossing from Las Palmas to St Lucia.

BOC AROUND ALONE

A four-stage solo round the world race run every four years. The 1982–3, 1986–7, 1990–91 and 1994–5 events were sponsored by British industrial and medical gasses conglomerate BOC.

CHS

Channel Handicap System – an Anglo-French rating rule pitched at mainstream cruiser-racers. Its low cost and simple measurement procedures have been adopted by many countries.

ILC

International Level Class – an elite level rating class under the complex IMS (International Measurement System) whereby different yachts comply with a common performance matrix to race without handicapping.

IMS

International Measurement System – grew out of a 1970s Massachusetts Institute of Technology project in which computer codes predict the speed potential of yachts. In 1992 it became the world wide common rule for measuring and rating offshore racing yachts.

IOR

International Offshore Rule – post World War II there was no common currency for offshore racing, but in 1969 the British Royal Ocean Racing Club and the Cruising Club of America merged their rules to form the IOR. Superceded in 1992 by IMS.

LOA

Length Overall – the length of a yacht from stem to stern. In the old days when bowsprits were the norm, a yacht's length was often expressed as LOD (Length on Deck) to exclude the bowsprit.

LWL

Load Waterline – strictly speaking, the length of the hull immersed in the water when a boat is floating in her loaded state. Nowadays used to refer to simply as waterline length.

MORC

Midget Offshore Racing Championship – popular low grade handicapping rule used in the USA and Canada for smaller racers in the 1960s and '70s

PHRF

Performance Handicap Rating Factor – simple, crude but popular American handicap rule aimed at weekend racers.

RORC

Royal Ocean Racing Club – cornerstone of offshore racing around the world. Founded in 1925 in the immediate aftermath of the very first Fastnet Race.

OSTAR

Observer Singlehanded Transatlantic Race – first run from Plymouth, England, to Newport-Rhode Island in 1960, having been created by "Blondie" Hasler. Sir Francis Chichester was an early competitor. Initial sponsorship by *The Observer* was superceded by Carlsberg (hence C-STAR) and a French radio station (Europe-1 STAR).

SARDINIA CUP

A Mediterranean event which alternates with the Admiral's Cup, based on Sardinia's north-eastern tip where HH Aga Khan developed the Costa Smeralda and the town of Porto Cervo.

SYDNEY–HOBART RACE

One of the world's great ocean races, founded in 1945, by British sailor and designer, Captain John Illingworth, later one of the five donors of the Admiral's Cup. It starts inside Sydney harbour every Boxing Day.

VENDÉE GLOBE

Probably the world's most severe yacht race: a solo, non-stop race around the world. Founded by Frenchman Philippe Jeantot, it alternates with the BOC/Around Alone race, which he won twice. The start and finish is in Les Sables d'Olonne, a fishing port in the Vendée region of France's Biscay coast.

VPP

Velocity Prediction Program – a computer code which assesses the design characteristics of a yacht and calculates the speed potential at different sailing angles and in different wind speeds.